P9-DBZ-978

66 SQUARE FEET

{ A DELICIOUS LIFE }

One Woman, One Terrace, 92 Recipes

MARIE VILJOEN

STEWART, TABORI & CHANG | NEW YORK

Published in 2013 by Stewart, Tabori & Chang
An imprint of ABRAMS

Text copyright © 2013 Marie Viljoen
Photographs copyright © 2013 Marie Viljoen, except images on back cover,
pages 16–17, 21, 23, 24, 32–33, 48–49, 64–65, 82–83, 120–121, 138–139,
142–143, 154–155, 174–175, 188–189, 206–207, 210, 211, copyright © 2013
Vincent Mounier

All rights reserved. No portion of this book may be reproduced, stored in a
retrieval system, or transmitted in any form or by any means, mechanical,
electronic, photocopying, recording, or otherwise, without written permission
from the publisher.

Cataloging-in-Publication Data has been applied for and may be obtained
from the Library of Congress.

ISBN: 978-1-61769-050-1

Editor: Dervla Kelly
Designer: Anna Christian
Production Manager: Tina Cameron

The text of this book was composed in Adobe Caslon and Bryant.
Printed and bound in the U.S.A.

10 9 8 7 6 5 4 3 2 1

Stewart, Tabori & Chang books are available at special discounts when
purchased in quantity for premiums and promotions as well as fundraising
or educational use. Special editions can also be created to specification.
For details, contact specialsales@abramsbooks.com or the address below.

ABRAMS
THE ART OF BOOKS SINCE 1949

115 West 18th Street
New York, NY 10011
www.abramsbooks.com

3 9222 03111 900 6

TO MY MOTHER, MAUREEN VILJOEN
FOR FEEDING ME, AND FOR TEACHING
ME THE NAMES OF FLOWERS

contents

introduction

I have always looked at what is growing at my feet to know where and when I am in the world. And then I have tried to eat it.

In New York, a city more famous for its concrete and culture than for its plants, I see green. I find wild violets and edible knotweed shoots in Central Park's Ramble in April and notice the English roses on a Brooklyn fence in May as a cab rushes by. I take note of rhubarb and ramps arriving at farmers' markets. In June I pick ripe serviceberries beside the Hudson and East rivers. On the street I photograph cherry tomatoes hanging from a fire escape in August. I water my own heirloom tomatoes on the roof of our apartment. I pick meadow mushrooms and eat them on toast in September, and in October there are maitake in Green-Wood Cemetery.

For me, New York City is an unfolding, edible calendar.

This fabled place is one whose contradictions of wealth and poverty, ostentation and decay, visible congestion and personal isolation, lure of success and specter of failure, conspire to chew a person up and spit her out if a way is not found to make peace with them.

Our tiny urban lullwater, a very small terrace fringed with green above the never-resting street, is where I am able to press pause and shut out the noise.

I was born very far from New York in a small city called Bloemfontein in a kidney-shaped province called the Free State in the middle of South Africa. *Bloemfontein* means flower fountain. I grew up in a high-walled garden in placid suburbia in a city dotted with low, grassy hills called *koppies*.

In Bloemfontein I was given a narrow strip of earth behind the house, beside the enclosures and cages where my brothers kept songbirds, quails, and ducks, and where we shared guinea pigs and rabbits. I sowed my first seeds there—radishes. I planted muscari, sweet peas, and ixias. My mother's herb and vegetable gardens grew nearby and later expanded to an acquired piece of land next door, where she made a terraced vegetable garden. Fruit grew all over the garden: plums, apricots, peaches, figs, gooseberries, and youngberries. Picking fresh chervil or a ripe plum, collecting green beans or a bunch of flowers, was a way of life, and exciting. Food and flowers were living things, from real places and plants.

My childhood birthday in October coincided with the first blooming of the roses in my mother's rose garden, and I still associate that day with the image of a perfectly round and delicate pink glass vase of roses on my birthday table, filled with fragrant blooms—Peace, Pappa Meilland, Double Delight—surrounded by frosted cupcakes, wobbling jellies, and plates of cookies, baked for a sit-down birthday feast.

☙

I grew up with good food. My mother is still the best cook I know, and she makes each meal a gastronomic experience. I remember her teaching me to stir béchamel in that kitchen, for cheese sauce to pour over cauliflower or broccoli, and how I was allowed to lick the saucy wooden spoon where pepper and salt had accumulated near the handle. I made the gravy for our every-other-Sunday roast—beef, lamb, or pork—stirring up the pan juices, adding wine and cream, and a brown powder from a box called Bisto (it was later banished). On the Sundays in between we *braaied* (barbecued), my father turning lamb chops and *boerewors* (sausages) over the coals beside the swimming pool.

When I was twelve, my father decided he'd outgrown his professional legal environment, and our family moved to Cape Town so he could pursue his career at the Cape Town Bar. For my mother, this was a return, at last, to the city where she had spent a happy childhood, playing under pine trees and pretending to be Christopher Robin. In Cape Town, a foreign and dramatic landscape replaced the grasslands and hills and corn fields of the Free State. Mountains serrated with vineyards and covered in indigenous *fynbos* loomed above strings of gleaming white and rocky beaches.

As a fourteen-year-old in Cape Town, in a new garden with no walls and a spectacular view of Table Mountain's green eastern flank, I laid out my mother's first formal herb garden and I began to immerse myself in books about edible plants, herbs, and wildflowers.

The first serious cooking I attempted was in Cape Town, when I was fourteen. My mother had caught chicken pox from me and was very ill. From her bed, for two weeks, she dictated the evening meals to me. It was a crash course in good cooking. The first dish I ever cooked was braised short ribs with juniper berries and bay leaves. The next was roast chicken.

Every September, until I left South Africa, we held a big garden party called the Spring Breakfast. My mother, assisted by Tipsy Titoti, our wonderful housekeeper, would cook for days to stock a massive buffet table with potted prawns, terrines and pâtés with homemade bread, several soups, poached salmon trout, mounds of asparagus spears, fluffy savory cheesecakes, a huge pot of lamb-with-a-spoon, cooked for a day, chocolate tarts, and heaps of strawberries. I contributed desserts and superfluous handmade chocolate truffles and made-from-scratch puff pastry pigs' ears. Orange juice and sparkling wine flowed in a river of Buck's Fizz, and pink umbrellas dotted the garden like giant flowers, in among the blossoming crab apples, jewel-like *vygies*, and indigenous blooming bulbs, all wrapped in the heavy scent of jasmine growing on the fence.

As the spindly young plane tree in the fledgling garden grew, ambitious weekend meals were eaten in its shade. Trestle tables and stray chairs were pulled together and friends stayed for long, bibulous lunches. Cats and dogs stretched out nearby. Recently a deck was built beneath the huge tree to accommodate over a dozen for a meal of many courses beneath the rustling canopy of ventilated shade in the hottest of summers in that beautiful garden.

I had caught the cooking bug hard, thanks to my mother's chicken pox, and began cooking my way methodically through her kitchen library, starting innocently enough with hardcore French technique cookbooks bought on overseas trips during which my parents ate at restaurants bristling with Michelin stars: the brothers Roux and Troisgros, Roger Vergé, Paul Bocuse, Raymond and Georges Blanc, Nico Ladenis, Marco Pierre White. I made terrines and mousses and soufflés and tarts and consommés and puff pastries and reductions and served forth eight-course dinner parties, whirling around the kitchen like a fiend, the unflappable Tipsy as my sous chef and stager.

My mother's great teacher, also from books, had been Elizabeth David, the English author who brought the light of French provincial cooking to the boil-everything British. And so I read her, too, and still do. My mother gave me David's first cookbook, which my father had given to her and in which he inscribed: *Not for instruction, but for inspiration.* And hers is the sort of food we ate most often at home, and which probably still informs my cooking at an unconscious level. Reading Elizabeth David's work is an immersive experience—and enormously pleasurable—and influences my approach to cooking the food from any country, as I take a deep breath and allow the cultural waters to close over my head, in order to capture the thing that makes that food what it is, and to speak with its accent.

These cooks, and the others that followed, taught me—and I did not realize it at the time—not only *how* to cook, but how to think about living. In the introductions to their books the chefs spoke memorably, longingly, of eating locally grown fresh produce long before it became an activist fashion and legitimate cause of the early twenty-first century. My mother's edible gardens and Tipsy's wild plant grazing reinforced their philosophy. Kitchens, gardens, plants, and pleasure were intimately connected.

I left South Africa to pursue a career in opera and lived up and down the East Coast, from DC to New Haven, working briefly in Germany, before gravitating naturally to New York. A bad bout of whooping cough at a vulnerable emotional point in my life and a delicate stage of my singing career prompted me to throw in the towel, and I set my sights on gardens again. I became a rooftop garden designer and returned to plants, my first love, learning about local conditions as I went.

When I moved to my tiny apartment with an attached terrace it was the first time in my New York life that I was able to keep my plants on something larger than a windowsill. It was thrilling.

It also meant I could now cook over charcoal outside, essential for any South African to whom *braaing* is second to breathing. I could eat a sunlit breakfast or dinner beneath the New York stars and high winking plane lights. At night I could sleep while enjoying the breeze that flowed in from the wide-open door that led to the enclosed and private little garden. I became intimately acquainted with the changeable city skies. The New York sky is beautiful. From above the tiny rectangle open to the weather rain falls, snow floats down, the sun blazes, clouds loom and diminish. The terrace faces east and I still greet the rising of the sun over this most storied of cities with a lump in my throat.

I started a blog to share the life of the terrace. I was writing long emails home to my mother, often about my little garden, or about what I was cooking, and I had just bought my first digital camera. I was realizing that the process of documenting the smallnesses of botanical and domestic life was as absorbing and exciting to me as capturing the bigger New York picture.

I called the blog *66 Square Feet*, after measuring the length and width of my terrace carefully. As a designer of rooftop gardens within a high-end Manhattan real estate scene, I knew that square feet dominated city conversation. And that my square feet were laughable. The subtitle—*New York, One Woman, One Terrace, 12 Seasons*—was my ambiguous battle cry: Bring it on, I have a terrace! This new act of daily publishing connected me instantly to a larger world, and showed my small world to that large one. The sense of connection was like being plugged into something, and a light came on.

My inaugural blog post was about a party I threw for the May terrace roses, which were in heavy bloom. Friends came and drank Bellinis and ate little crustless sandwiches. They could not all fit on the terrace at once and had to revolve in and out. Writing about the garden and posting its pictures was a way of inviting more people in, and of sharing my great delight in small things with readers who seemed to take equal pleasure in them. I began to feel happier than I had for many years. Here I felt that I was able to live large, with little.

In my grown-up life in Brooklyn, with a 66-square-foot terrace, the grand scale of childhood has been telescoped to the bare minimum. Despite its constraints, this space has managed to be both a refuge from the teeming energy of the city and a source of inspiration and ingredients for my daily domestic life. A garden and a kitchen—regardless of scale—are my necessities.

❧

The act of cooking has satisfied the hedonist in me; it is an act that gives pleasure. But it has also provided direction, occupation, and a sense of achievement when my life has been unhappy, method when structure has been needed. It has been a practical form of escapism, masking my tendency to withdraw. It has consummated celebrations in happy times and has always been a reward to look forward to at the end of a day. Cooking now is less about following recipes than about imagination, memory, desire, and inspiration; the latter often grows on the terrace outside, on the roof above my head, or is brought back from the day's market or a foraging trip. In one dish I try to create a small pocket of perfection, an unassailable space in time when giving and taking pleasure in the present is the only goal.

Even if it is just melted cheese on toast.

While much of the food in this book is presented in menu form, be assured that we do not sit down to eat four or five courses every night. Any recipe can be taken from its context and enjoyed in its own right. At home in Brooklyn a typical meal for us includes a salad, a main dish, and wine, and I usually eat fruit afterwards, a habit learned from my father, who always chooses the least promising specimen first—one with a bruise, perhaps, because he knows no one else will eat it—and peels it carefully with a very sharp pocketknife.

The menus here are celebrations of a season, a month, an ingredient. Many of the recipes are old favorites—dishes to which I return again and again. Menus and dinner parties also speak to the lost charm of the shared table. I believe strongly in sitting down at a table to eat, even if the table is a cloth spread on the floor. It forces us to be still, to listen, to look into someone's eyes, to see them, to share something good, something in common.

KITCHEN NOTES

These meals were cooked in a very small kitchen.

Our kitchen's length, if I may use that ambitious word, is ten feet. Between the sink and the stove is a short counter, eighteen inches long and just as deep, where I keep a large chopping board. That is essentially my work surface. Behind the chopping board live my four staples: salt, sugar, pepper, and extra-virgin olive oil. My one kitchen appliance is beside them—a blender. There is a small storage cupboard above the stove in which I keep a spice collection that allows me to summon up with ease the food of the cultures and countries I love. I keep other essentials there: unscented oils, cans of good tuna, coconut milk, tomato paste, bottles of honey and homemade jams and anchovies, boxes of cocoa and crackers and pasta and dried fruit, and a small basket of garlic, potatoes, and shallots. And cat treats. On the tiny piece of counter at the far end of the kitchen are the infused alcohols, the day's loaf of fresh bread, my knives. The cupboards below hold a collection of pots. And there is a tiny dishwasher.

The fridge is permanently stocked with tamarind paste, fish sauce, and lemongrass. Southeast Asia in the house. Then there are soy, tahini, at least two vinegars, mustard, capers, cornichons, eggs, butter, cheese, and nonfat milk. There are always lemons. Running out of sour citrus makes me tremble with nervousness. A small supply of vegetables and fruit lives in the lower reaches, along with bottles of homemade pickles and relishes and syrups.

Finally, there is the living and variable larder on the terrace and roof farm. Depending on the season, the herbs I am able to use daily include thyme, rosemary, marjoram, sage, tarragon, chives, mint, parsley, basil, fennel, cilantro, summer savory, and shiso. There are strawberries from May until November, a brief week of blueberries, white currants, and black raspberries, and late summer figs. The roof produces wonderful summer tomatoes as well as cucumbers, peppers, and eggplants. There are salad leaves in the cooler seasons and parsnips in winter.

While I sometimes dream of an airy place to cook, with tall windows and a long solid kitchen table around which I can gather friends and hungry strays, I know that I am lucky to have a tiny garden, an enterprising spirit, and access to the world's most diverse markets to help satisfy my hunger for beautiful food and thoughtful meals.

PICNIC NOTES

If a picnic is packed properly it can transport you quite efficiently, for a few hours, to a vacation within spitting distance of home. A good picnic is a state of mind.

I have only one rule: ACCEPT NO PLASTIC. It is unspecial. The sound of a fork against plastic is a dull, depressing thunk.

Pack real glasses. They may be cheap, but they must be glass. Size doesn't matter. You can refill them as much as you like.

You need a tablecloth, for the grass, or bench, and something else to sit on.

Cloth napkins (you can roll the glasses and flatware in them).

Real knives and forks.

A small and very sharp cutting knife. I love Opinel. Vince loves Victorinox.

A small cutting board for cutting bread and cheese, and for balancing small dishes of things.

Pretty plates. I use pressed tin plates I found at The Metropolitan Museum of Art Store. Sidewalk sales, Chinatown, and camping supply stores offer wonderful enameled tin plates and bowls.

Cold wine or drinks. Find and buy a freezer sleeve that hugs your bottle.

Mason jars for patés, butter, salad dressings, and salt and pepper.

Thermos flasks or old wine bottles for transporting soup, to be sipped from glasses.

JANUARY

NEW YORK IN JANUARY

Average temperatures: 39°F / 26°F (4°C / -3°C)

January, despite its paralyzing cold, is always a beginning.

For me, it is the month when my married life in New York began, with my husband's green card interview. Since meeting Vincent (a citizen of both France and Canada) two and a half years before in the cyberspace between Vancouver, Canada, and New York City, and realizing very quickly that He Was the One, this day had been looming. It had not been easy. Despite having been married for two years already, we had been living obediently on opposite coasts, in neighboring countries, enjoying the thrill of meeting at monthly intervals but increasingly weary of the red tape that is tangled around the Immigration and Naturalization Service. We were in limbo.

It was our task to prove to the INS that we were married because we were in love, and to that end we supplied the INS with the *War and Peace* of paperwork: the very first comments we ever left for each other after I stumbled upon his website, the long, thrilled e-mails we began to exchange a month later, the pictures and blog posts from our first in-person meeting and all subsequent contact. It was the most documented of love affairs. Postcards, photos, missives from happy and concerned friends responding to my mass e-mail informing them of our intention to marry within months of meeting—one entreating me: "What exactly is your rush?"—and sworn affidavits, the one from my lawyer-father starting in South African legalese: "I am a major white South African male . . ."

No argument there. But I hadn't laughed so hard for a long time.

There were wedding pictures. There were pictures of picnics on New York and Cape Town beaches, Namibian sand dunes, in Canadian snowdrifts. There were receipts: for wedding rings and plane tickets. There were phone bills, electrical bills, bank statements. The litter of love.

We celebrated with dim sum and cold beer in nearby Chinatown, giddy with relief.

Chinatown has always been my winter habit. The miasma of summer's astonishing street smells is obliterated by the rigid cold. The metal light of

January reveals repeated heaps of rioting tropical produce—curved yellow mangos, lychees and longans in brown bunches, wiry red mangosteens, palm-sized papayas nestling in tissue paper, poles of purple sugar cane—reminding me that this is the city where the planet and its appetites converge. After shopping for sun-filled fruit and bunches of garlic chives we retire to Dim Sum Go Go for their delicate dumplings. On the tables a triumvirate of condiment dishes waits as it always does: the freshly grated green ginger, chewy, addictive XO sauce, and sweet vinegar in small white dishes are forever associated with cold hands, long walks, and a sense of exhilaration. The thought of the juicy roast duck dumplings to come makes life seem impossibly sweet. After lunch we stop at a fishmonger on Grand Street and buy our once-a-year Dungeness crabs, and walk them home over the Brooklyn Bridge.

This is the rare month, the only month, when I cannot tell time by what is in bloom. The botanical city is on lockdown. Street trees are naked, the sidewalks are tight-lipped and weed-free. Discarded Christmas trees cast adrift on curbs weep dry needles, waiting for trash pickup. Concrete and metal and rust and empty earth are laid bare. The city is stripped. The only thing in bloom on the exposed streets is graffiti, which comes into its own: sharks swim up chain-link fences in Red Hook, women warriors wander lost in Dumbo, rats wrestle on Spring Street, and memories of political dreams peel near the Bowery, where Obama still wears his superman cape. A truck's tattooed and tagged side lights up a dirty snowdrift on nearby Forsyth Street.

Out on Jamaica Bay the small islands in the water are encased in rime and frost. The edges of ponds are frozen and ice entombs the last red berries on autumn olive branches. The Jamaica Bay Wildlife Refuge has been flattened and smoothed under a layer of snow that dusts the pale beaches with white, frosting even the low-tide mud. In the sepia landscape of brown branches and bleached reeds the cordgrass appears as a bright highlight under a sky that holds more snow.

Tuned to the subtleties of cold, in January we walk. Up on the Brooklyn Heights Promenade we head into a bleeding 4:45 P.M. sun setting across the water over Jersey. Below us the small waves of New York Harbor leave icicles suspended from the rocks and bollards lining the Brooklyn shore. I leave Vincent in the gathering dark above the Brooklyn-Queens Expressway, taking panoramic shots of Manhattan as traffic thunders below. Daylight is swallowed by the afternoon dark and lights appear in the rising monoliths of the Financial District across the East River.

I move toward home, stopping on my way to buy ingredients for a fiery one-pot supper, and a couple of cold beers. Once the sun has left the city it is too cold to stand still.

Crabs with Black Bean Sauce

Sweet crabmeat and salty beans are fingerlicking good. You need the freshest of crabs, and I buy mine live. I can only face murdering them once a year. A wok or very wide pan is best to accommodate the chopped-up sections of crab. Two finger bowls of piping hot water with lemon are a good idea, as well as claw crackers and napkins the size of bedsheets. Accompany with cold beer.

« SERVES FOUR »

2 fresh or live large Dungeness crabs

¼ cup (45 g) salted black beans

¼ cup (60 ml) soy sauce

¼ cup (60 ml) coconut or unscented oil

1 thumb-size piece of ginger, peeled and sliced into matchsticks

4 cloves garlic, sliced into matchsticks

2 teaspoons sugar

Juice of 1 lemon

1 teaspoon hot chile flakes or 1 small whole, fresh, hot red chile, finely chopped

⅓ cup (80 ml) cold water with ¼ teaspoon cornstarch stirred into it

4 scallions, white and green parts finely sliced

Fill a pot large enough to accommodate the crabs with water and bring to a boil. Meanwhile, place the crabs in the freezer for 20 minutes to put them to sleep. Plunge them into the boiling water, clap the pot lid on, and boil for 8 minutes. Remove the crabs, rinse under cold water, and drain.

Pull off the hard carapace and take out the dead man's fingers, which are the crab's gills. Also remove the gritty stomach sack, below the eyes. The worst part is now over. Cut the crabs in half, and then into quarters. Crack each leg with the back of the knife or cleaver, so that the sauce can penetrate during cooking.

In a small bowl, mash the black beans with the soy sauce, leaving some beans intact. Heat the oil in a wok or large sauté pan over medium heat. Add the ginger and garlic, cooking gently for 2 to 3 minutes to scent the oil. Do not brown the garlic or it will be bitter. Add the black bean–soy sauce paste, sugar, lemon juice, and chile, stirring well to mix. Add the cornstarch slurry and stir. Turn the heat to high and quickly add the crab pieces, tossing and turning continuously until heated through and coated with sauce.

Top with the scallions and serve straight from the wok or from a large bowl. A side of rice, eaten from individual bowls, is always a good idea. Finish the meal with whole mangoes or a platter of tropical fruit.

Terence Hill's Beans

My brothers, Anton and Francois, watched spaghetti Westerns with their friends on their birthdays. That is how I fell in love with Terence Hill at the age of six, and why I wanted to be a cowboy . . .

In the movie *My Name is Nobody* Terence Hill, as Nobody, eats beans. Twice. Those blue eyes in that brown face and his sloppy, happy, wooden-spoon-and-ladle eating inspired me to make these beans for him. Nobody would want to make beans for prissy Henry Fonda.

This makes about four solitary meals or can be split among friends. For a vegan version, omit the pancetta and use mushroom stock.

Sour cream on top is good, too.

⫷ SERVES FOUR ⫸

- 2 cups (365 g) uncooked red kidney beans
- 2 tablespoons olive oil
- 6 slices pancetta, cut crosswise into ribbons
- 1 bunch scallions, white and green parts, sliced
- 5 cloves garlic, crushed lightly, skins removed
- 2 medium carrots, finely chopped
- 2 stalks celery, finely sliced
- 3 tablespoons tomato paste
- 3 cups (720 ml) chicken stock
- 2 teaspoons brown sugar
- 2 Poblano peppers, soaked, seeded, and roughly chopped
- 6 sprigs thyme
- 1 bunch parsley
- 1 tablespoon red wine vinegar
- 1 cup (240 ml) dry but fruity red wine, such as a shiraz
- Salt
- Freshly ground black pepper
- Rolls, for serving
- Unsalted butter, for serving

Soak the beans in water overnight or bring to a boil and allow to rest in water until cool. Discard the soaking water. In a large pan over medium heat, heat the olive oil. Add the pancetta and cook until some of the fat has been rendered.

Add the scallions, garlic, carrots, and celery and sauté for about 5 minutes. Add the tomato paste and stir until it has lightly caramelized, about 1 minute. Add the beans, with enough chicken stock or water to cover them. Add the sugar, peppers, and herbs. Stir to combine, then cover and simmer until the beans are fork-tender, adding additional stock or water from time to time as needed. When the beans are barely tender, still a little chewy, add the vinegar and red wine. Cook, uncovered, until the wine has been absorbed. Taste and add salt and freshly ground black pepper as needed.

Serve hot with warm rolls and butter. Not that Nobody had either.

THE
JANUARY
TERRACE

What I notice now is not the terrace itself but what lies beyond it. On a sunny day in the thin air of January, the intensely blue sky is an enormous presence. It is this illusion of limitlessness that makes our life in such a small space possible. The variable sky becomes a theater, ushering in panoramas of cloud, etched contrails, a seamless expanse entered only by silent jets flying at cruising altitude, dim silver objects moving at 30,000 feet and beyond to places we imagine or already know, or low, heavy, miraculous machines on their final and weightless approach to LaGuardia and JFK in front of us, to the east, or Newark International behind us, to the west. When the wind is right, we hear the roar of their takeoff, the restrained power of their descent.

To the northeast lies the stepped skyline of downtown Brooklyn. Dead east is a church steeple, copper green and slender above waves of brownstone and townhouse rooftops. To the south is another church steeple, a brown castle with medieval stone turrets now damaged by a fatal lightning strike, and far beyond that a faint hill, pale brown in the horizon's winter haze. That is Green-Wood Cemetery. The winterbare points of tall street trees punctuate the spaces in between. To look west, and see the water of New York Harbor, we must stand on the terrace's stone table to look out and over our own silvertop roof, or climb the ladder on the landing and pop the hatch that leads to it. But in January the roof hatch remains shut. The pots of the roof farm above our heads slumber in the cold. Somewhere deep in their soil, I hope that my parsnips are still growing.

This is the big sleep, the rare month when nothing happens. Consequently, it is a useful month for travel. It is hard for a gardener to leave the garden, but the suspended life of the wizened January terrace gives me permission to go, and we fly far south, some 8,000 miles, to visit my parents in sunny South Africa, two seasons and a hemisphere away, to walk and eat in that other garden, my mother's, which taught me so much of what I know.

When we return everything is still dormant, thanks to the preserving cold. The month when nothing moves is a rare and welcome pause.

In terms of the kitchen, the best thing about January is precisely and perversely what makes winter unbearable to those who flee the city for longer days under a higher sun: the cold. It is freezing outside and I make the most of it by warming the apartment as much as I like with long, introspective cooking. Multiple courses of hot dishes are possible, something unthinkable in summer. An additional perk is that our heating bill is nonexistent.

The dark and cold conspire to make me crave sauces, starch, and slow-cooked foods spiced with nostalgia. I want to eat from deep bowls and dip bread into soup.

Bear Talk

January is apple country. Hard cider seems a sensible seasonal drink, and I add a dash of Cognac to make a seasonal apéritif. Sometimes the cognac has been infused with the lemony flavor of the previous fall's spicebush berries.

If I were a bear, woken and grumpy in the middle of winter, I would want to drink this. A small barrelful.

Enjoy the party. Just don't wake the bear . . .

≪ MAKES ONE DRINK ≫

1 ounce (2 tablespoons) Cognac	4 ounces (8 tablespoons) hard apple cider

Pour the Cognac into a coupe and top with the well-chilled cider.

cold weather dinner

Bear Talk

Borscht Consommé

White Winter Salad

Chicken with Olives

Crème Caramel

Borscht Consommé

Borscht is probably the most famous—or notorious—incarnation of hated or loved beets. I love them and I love it. Hot or cold, hearty or austere, it is a gorgeous soup. There are countless versions: with pieces of meat and vegetables and big white beans in it, it is a stand-alone and filling meal.

This is a lighter dinner party version, clear and bright red, the essence of borscht. Consommés are an elegant and deceptively simple vehicle for intense flavor. For a gutsier meal, add two short ribs on the bone and cook an extra hour, then shred the meat.

⟪ SERVES SIX ⟫

1 tablespoon olive oil

5 strips pancetta or good bacon, cut crosswise into 1-inch (2.5 cm) pieces

1 large onion, thinly sliced

6 beets, peeled and grated, stems and leaves reserved and roughly chopped

4 cloves garlic, thinly sliced

1 bulb fennel with fronds, roughly chopped

1 large carrot, peeled, halved, and sliced crosswise into half moons

2 stalks celery, thinly sliced

8 whole juniper berries, lightly crushed

5 whole allspice berries

4 bay leaves

1 tablespoon whole black peppercorns

Small bunch parsley

8 sprigs thyme, tied in a bundle with cooking twine

2 tablespoons sugar

½ teaspoon salt

8 cups (2 L) chicken stock

3 tablespoons red wine vinegar

Lemon juice

2 egg whites, gently whisked

6 tablespoons (85 g) sour cream, for serving

In a large saucepan over medium heat, heat the oil. Add the pancetta or bacon and sauté gently until its fat is rendered. Add the onions and cover the pan for 5 minutes to encourage sweating. Cook gently and slowly until the onions are golden with brown bits, at least 10 minutes more. Add the rest of vegetables and the berries. Stir. Add the juniper, allspice, bay leaves, peppercorns, parsley, thyme, sugar, salt, stock, and vinegar and stir to combine. Bring to a boil, then lower to a simmer and skim off any foam that rises. Cook, uncovered, for about 45 minutes, until the vegetables are beyond tender. Taste and add more salt if necessary. Add a squeeze of lemon juice.

Strain the liquid through a sieve into a large bowl, pressing all the juice from the vegetables. Return the broth to the pot and simmer until reduced by a quarter, about 45 minutes. Taste and add more salt if necessary. Remove from the heat and allow the soup to cool. For a crystal-clear consommé, add the whisked egg white to the cooled, concentrated liquid and bring it back to a boil. The egg white will coagulate and catch any sediment floating around. Strain through a piece of muslin into a bowl.

Divide the consommé among six bowls and top each with 1 tablespoon sour cream.

White Winter Salad

In January I have not yet begun to resent root vegetables.

Pale and interesting have always appealed to me. I first ate an all-white salad at Al Di La, where I have loved to eat since I moved to Brooklyn. They treat salads with respect. And without salad in some form, my life is incomplete. Here, raw root vegetables are the stars. Collect as many different kinds of white or pale roots, tubers, and stems as you can find: parsnips, rutabagas, turnips, kohlrabi, radishes, sunchokes, salsify, celeriac, fennel, celery hearts. Sweet apples—Honeycrisp are perfect—and bright pomegranate seeds make the pale salad sparkle.

《 SERVES SIX 》

FOR THE SALAD

5 cups (550 g) very thinly sliced mixed white vegetables (see Note)

1 apple, cored, thinly sliced, and sprinkled with lemon juice

FOR THE LEMON JUICE AND HAZELNUT OIL VINAIGRETTE

2 tablespoons fresh lemon juice

Salt

¼ teaspoon sugar

Freshly ground black pepper

5 tablespoons (75 ml) hazelnut or walnut oil

TO SERVE

2 heads of Belgian endive, leaves separated

⅓ cup (60 g) pomegranate seeds

Note: Cut the larger vegetables into slivers or batons—mixing up the shapes adds appeal to the salad.

Set the white vegetable and apple slices aside in a large bowl while you prepare the lemon juice and hazelnut oil vinaigrette.

In a large mixing bowl, just before serving, whisk the lemon juice with salt to taste and the sugar until they are dissolved. Add pepper to your tastes (I like a lot). Whisk in the oil until the dressing is lightly emulsified.

Using your hands, gently toss the white vegetables and apple slices in the mixing bowl until they are covered with dressing. Heap the salad in the middle of a serving plate with the endive either in among the vegetables and fruit or arranged around the edges. Scatter the pomegranate seeds over top and serve at once.

Chicken with Olives

This powerful and rustic stew has become a household favorite for cold weather. It evolved by happy accident one night when I did not feel like leaving the apartment to shop. I had chicken in the fridge, but little else. I scoured what passes for a larder and came up with garlic, a shallot, a tube of tomato paste, hot Aleppo pepper, and bay leaves. I added the remnants of a Syrian olive mix to make it look more interesting, and mustard as an afterthought. It is good served with wide noodles. This is what you might eat if Sicily and Syria and France collided. If you hate warm olives, as I used to, omit them, but this dish may just convert you, as it did me. On no account should you leave out the mustard.

⫷ SERVES SIX ⫸

1 tablespoon olive oil

3 shallots, thinly sliced

1 head garlic, cloves separated and skins removed

¼ cup (60 ml) tomato paste

6 chicken legs-and-thighs (still attached) or 6 drumsticks and 6 thighs

2 cups (480 ml) dry, fruity white wine, such as a pinot grigio

2 tablespoons grainy mustard

1½ cups (200 g) good black and green olives (I leave them unpitted, but warn your guests)

2 teaspoons sugar

1 tablespoon Aleppo pepper or chile flakes

3 bay leaves

Salt

Freshly ground black pepper

1 pound (455 g) uncooked wide or large-shaped pasta, such as pappardelle or large shells

In a Dutch oven over medium heat, heat the oil. Add the shallots and sweat them, about 5 minutes. Add the garlic cloves and cook until they turn slightly golden, about 2 minutes. Add the tomato paste and stir. Cook for 1 minute—this caramelizes and sweetens the tomato paste.

Add the chicken, wine, mustard, olives, sugar, chile, bay leaves, and salt and pepper to taste.

Add water to barely cover the chicken pieces, cover, and bring to a boil. Lower the heat and cook at a simmer, covered, for an hour. Remove the lid, and simmer for another hour, until the chicken is very tender and the sauce has reduced. Taste for seasoning, adding more salt and pepper as necessary.

Fifteen minutes before the chicken is ready, cook the pasta according to the package directions. Drain it and return to the pot. Spoon the sauce from the chicken over the drained pasta just before serving. Toss. Distribute the noodles among 6 warm plates and top with the chicken pieces. Serve.

Crème Caramel

I love desserts that quiver. This is my mother's recipe, and it is still one of the best things she can make for one of her legendary Lunches Under the Tree in the middle of her garden in Cape Town. The bland, just-set custard is pushed over the edge into addictiveness by the suggestive taste of the burned sugar. It fills spaces you didn't know you had and its coolness is perfect after the fiery chicken.

My mother's handwritten instruction: "Give Recipe Your Undivided Attention." So I do.

Make this the day before you need it.

≪ SERVES SIX ≫

FOR THE CARAMEL	FOR THE CUSTARD	5 eggs	¼ teaspoon salt
½ cup (100 g) sugar	3 cups (720 ml) milk	⅓ cup (65 g) sugar	¼ teaspoon vanilla extract

Fill a roasting pan with ¾ inches (2 cm) of water, place it in the oven, and preheat the oven to 300°F (150°C).

Make the caramel: In a heavy saucepan over medium heat, melt the sugar for the caramel until it is amber. Do not allow it to burn. Pour the caramel into a warmed 2.5 quart (2.5 L) custard or soufflé dish and tilt to coat the bottom evenly. Allow to cool completely.

Make the custard: Heat the milk in a saucepan until small bubbles rise at the sides. In a large bowl, beat the eggs until the yolks and whites have blended. Stir in the sugar and the salt. Pour the hot milk onto the egg mixture while stirring, making sure the sugar and salt have dissolved. Add the vanilla extract. Pour the mixture into the custard dish. Tap gently to dislodge bubbles at the sides.

Place the custard dish carefully into the pan of hot water and slide it very gently back into the oven. Bake the custard for 75 minutes or until a knife or skewer dipped into the custard comes out clean. Cool to room temperature and then chill in the refrigerator, covered, for at least 5 hours. Overnight is best.

When ready to serve, dip a knife in boiling water and slide it around the edges of the custard. Place a serving plate on top of the custard dish (make sure your serving plate has a slight lip to contain the sauce from the caramel). Invert the dishes in one quick movement, giving them a no-nonsense up-down shake. You should hear a satisfying plop. Place the serving plate on a flat surface and gently pull off the custard dish. The top of the custard will be a rich brown and sticky sauce will be running down the edges.

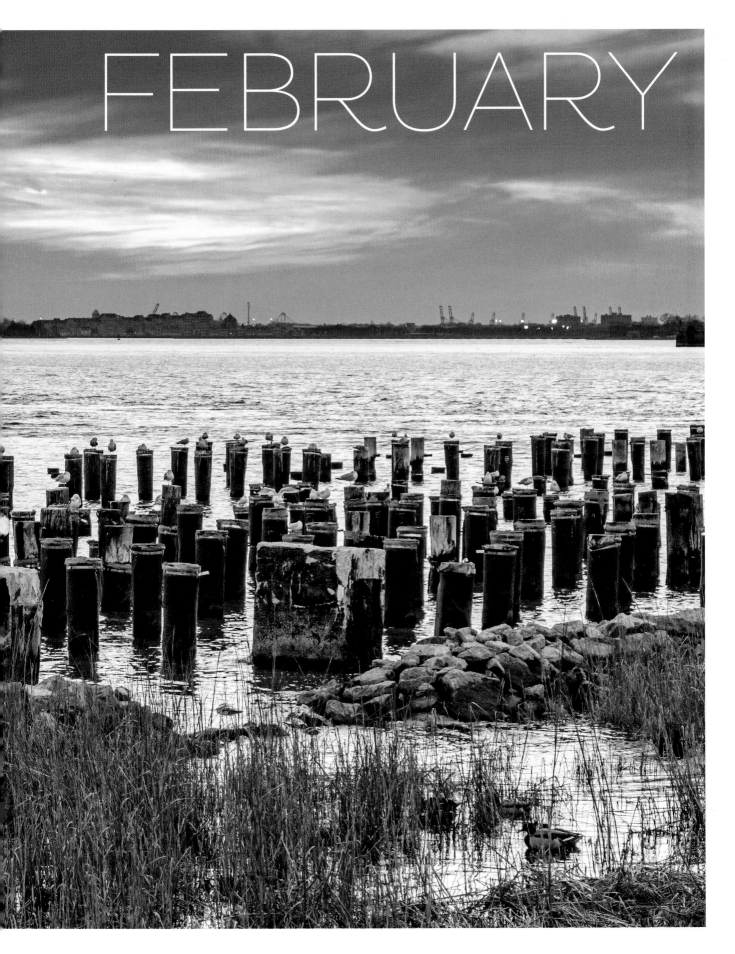

FEBRUARY

NEW YORK IN FEBRUARY

Average temperatures: 40°F / 27°F (4°C / -3°C)

The city is locked in uncompromising cold. On a clear day under a high blue sky with wind slicing through the sunlight, I walk out to meet winter, heavier by five pounds in clothes alone. I leave the house insulated in layers of cashmere beneath a heavy coat. Wool makes me itch. There are long socks under my tall boots. I wear a knitted cap down over my ears and a scarf is doubled around my throat and nose.

Snow has fallen. The spartan street trees of winter are snow-limbed and sumptuous, the uppermost lines of their dark branches draped in white. The bluestone sidewalk on nearby Congress Street has become a sparkling palace, an endless empty hall under frosted arches. I walk in the middle of the street and my boots squeak on the snow.

The frozen stall-keepers at the farmers' market preside over bins of root vegetables and apples. Week in, week out. I buy them anyway. Spiky green wheat grass grown for cats looks luscious and I carry some home with me for the terrace-deprived feline, my own mouth watering just a little.

Within the cold heart of the month unexpected flowers appear. Witch hazels ring in the February flower scene, blooming through hard freezes, their spidery streamers suspended improbably above snow. In Brooklyn Bridge Park near the tidal heave of the East River they are backlit, ablaze against a backdrop of dull skyscrapers.

At Cadman Plaza Park, where the path leads up to the Brooklyn Bridge, there is a pale yellow witch hazel whose flowers are an annual fluorescent foreground to the yellow cabs that pass beyond it, down the off-ramp from the humming metal bridge. In the dead leaves at its feet are bright winter aconite flowers, framed by minute Elizabethan collars of green. A few blocks away on the Brooklyn Promenade I find white hellebores, delicate under crystals of ice.

On Amity Street one evening I am stopped in my tracks by an intoxicating scent. Winter honeysuckle is not in bloom yet, so that does not explain it. There is a garden hidden behind a tall wall. Something is flowering in there.

I return, pushing a note written on good paper under the expensive door, "I smelled something wonderful behind your garden wall. What is it?" I include my e-mail address. The homeowner responds and tells me about the huge old witch hazel in the garden. She invites me to visit and watches me, politely bemused as I circle her tree. It is festooned with threads of electric yellow. Scent rises around from them, timid in daylight, growing in the dark. I had no idea.

Behind the rockery at the Brooklyn Botanic Garden the witch hazels flower in unison. 'Jelena' has a hot amber heart bleeding into warm yellow. 'James Wells' keeps its dead leaves until spring, not letting go of the furled dry cloaks until sure of the next best thing.

In bright, cold weather we visit the sea. Coney Island's boardwalk is empty and the peeling paint and bygone curlicues become picturesque in afternoon light like pale tea. This is not the summer scene when a tide of sticky humanity engulfs the doubtful beaches. The wind is icy and the empty sand is dotted with well-wrapped Russians in fur hats. Iron gates livid with fun-fair graffiti are drawn down over the boardwalk concessions. The turquoise Ferris wheel is frozen against the sky. At Nathan's we eat raw pink clams from a paper plate and drink cold beer, and watch the locals. This is no time for tourists.

For a daytime picnic we walk toward Red Hook, along Columbia Street, heading for a bench on a boardwalk over the water where we can see the Statue of Liberty frozen in New York Harbor. Fishermen hunch over their poles. We eat brown bread still warm from Sahadi's, with hunks of brie and dry sausage, crisp cornichons, and sweet bread and butter pickles from the roof farm's long-ago summer cucumbers. Our hands shiver around the cold wine glasses and we lean in toward each other. The water is busy with taxis and ferries, their wakes white shocks in the pewter water. We are silently homesick after a recent trip to South Africa and miss our brief, idyllic road trips there. The winter picnic is a chilly substitute for that warm camplife, and our remembering amplifies both experiences. Looking at this working waterway reminds me that we are in the city at the center of the world's imagination. We are what Walker Percy describes as certified. Not nowhere. Somewhere. We watch a cold duck paddling in place. We dip teaspoons into our chocolate *pots de crème.*

Restless for adventure one night, we leave the apartment in the subfreezing air and walk toward Dumbo, where the massive stone feet of the Manhattan Bridge dominate the cobblestones, the yellow lights of night reminding me that I love this city in the dark, and then on to Vinegar Hill, where my nose leads me, for a drink at the bar and then supper. We eat a silky chicken liver mousse, a sardine tart, and cannelloni stuffed with lamb, fennel, and currants, while waitresses bitch audibly in the background.

On the walk back to Cobble Hill an improbable Mardi Gras band marches out in front of us in the darkness, the musicians in coats and mittens, wheeling on cue, the music and brass and hustling drum raucous beneath the cacophony of the overhead subway that passes into Manhattan on the tracks high above the buildings and black streets, where icicles hang in the doorways.

Days pass and March approaches. The first crocuses emerge, transparent in the sunlight, a shiver of petals on a berm in the Brooklyn Botanic Garden, above Flatbush Avenue. They tilt the year delicately toward the pale idea of spring.

Picnic

Pots de Crème

Unlike traditional *pots de crème*, there are no eggs in these, nor is anything cooked. Nothing could be easier. In covered containers, they become a cold picnic treat, the outside chill keeping the cream cool as you travel.

‹‹ SERVES SIX ››

1 cup (240 ml) whipping cream	1 small bar of good dark chocolate (3 ounces / 85 grams)

Whip the cream.

Break the chocolate into pieces and melt it in a saucepan over very low heat. Properly, this is done in a metal bowl over simmering water, but if you watch the chocolate like a hawk there will be no overheating problems in the saucepan. The chocolate must melt to the point of imminent collapse, where, at the touch of a wooden spoon, it gives up its shape and melts. As soon as it reaches this point, turn off the heat. Stir it fast. Scrape it into the whipped cream and then mix it in completely with the whisk until all the lovely dark trails of chocolate in the white cream have blended into pale brown. Spoon into little cups or glasses for dessert. Chill.

A tablespoon of something alcoholic, mixed in once the chocolate and cream have met, is rarely a bad idea.

THE FEBRUARY TERRACE

There are over thirty pots on the tiny terrace and along its edge, filled with shrubs, climbers, and perennials, not counting the empty ones. They sit out there, hunched and cold, terra-cotta and fiberglass and metal, an essay in crisp leaves and brittle twigs.

Despite the garden's sullen appearance, there is work to do—root pruning and repotting—for the chives, the Japanese forest grass, the hosta, and the fig (again), whose roots are close-packed and need release and fresh soil.

And the strawberries. The original three everbearing plants (the cultivar is 'Fern') produced dozens of offspring via runners, and after my initial capitalist satisfaction at this high-interest return on my investment I became exasperated by their constant need to reproduce. I moved many plants to the roof, after giving others away. I divide the plants every winter.

The biggest job, and the most fraught with emotional turmoil, is hauling the fig from its fiberglass container to saw off an inch or more of its tightly wound roots. I know that it is anesthetized by the cold, and that the surgery with my vicious-toothed Felco saw will be painless, but I love this tree, which has come to represent what is possible and romantic in a small space—its tropical leaves in summer, its fruit ripening up here among the Brooklyn rooftops, its defiance of the climate. I worry annually that I am about to kill it. I heave and pull and saw and unwind the mat of roots that comes away. I pour in new dark brown potting soil, replace the smaller, shorn root ball, and water. And then I wait, and hope.

The roof farm sits empty and changeless above our heads, but in the last days of the month there are parsnips to pull. I pop the hatch to the silver top and inspect my overwintered crop. In the deep pots tender leaves have emerged through the bleached remains of their generous fall growth. This is precisely the time to collect them, or they will turn stringy. I prod the dark earth experimentally and I haul them up. They emerge white and long, bristling with little hairs and parsnip promise. I am a happy February farmer. They will be dinner.

FEBRUARY MENU

For dinner parties when the three square feet of kitchen counter space become less challenging than insanity-provoking, I move dishes waiting to cook to the terrace, where they remain chilled. Wine is either iced fetchingly in a snowdrift or left on the stone table in the cold night.

For anyone with a sensibility geared toward seasonal eating, the fourth month of root vegetables is becoming provocative. Fortunately these taproots, tubers, and rhizomes are also hugely versatile, and here I salute them.

Apple Cognac Punch

I love punch. It always feels like a party. Prepare the apples in Cognac 24 hours in advance. You can substitute bourbon or brandy. If serving to larger numbers for a big party, double the quantity, combine in a punch bowl, and float freshly sliced rounds of apple in the punch.

⟪ SERVES SIX ⟫

1 sweet apple, thinly sliced into rounds

1 cup (240 ml) Cognac

2 tablespoons sugar

3 strips of lemon peel, 3 inches (7.5 cm) long

2 bottles dry sparkling wine or Champagne

Combine the apple slices, Cognac, sugar, and lemon peel in a small bowl. Stir to dissolve the sugar and leave in the fridge overnight, covered. Chill the bottle of wine.

Ten minutes before serving, strain the Cognac into a beautiful chilled jug or carafe and gently pour in the sparkling wine. Cover and refrigerate until needed, and then pour into coupes.

snowy weather dinner

Apple Cognac Punch

Carrot and Cumin Soup

Beetroot and Parsnip Salad

Oxtail Stew

Buttermilk Mashed Potatoes

Baked Apples

Carrot and Cumin Soup

Use big, mature carrots for this soup. They are sweeter.

《 SERVES SIX 》

2 tablespoons olive oil

3 extra-large carrots, peeled and roughly chopped (4 to 5 cups / 510 to 640 g)

1 large onion, chopped

3 cloves garlic, peeled and smashed

2 teaspoons ground cumin, plus extra for dusting

1 teaspoon ground coriander

1 cup (240 ml) orange juice

5 cups (1.2 L) chicken or vegetable stock

⅓ cup (75 g) sour cream, plus extra for serving

Salt

Freshly ground black pepper

Squeeze of fresh lemon juice

In a large saucepan over medium heat, heat the olive oil. Sauté the carrots, onions, and garlic gently until the onions are pale gold, about 12 minutes. Add the cumin and coriander and stir for a minute to toast and coat the vegetables. Add the orange juice and stock and bring to a simmer. Cook until the carrot pieces are just tender, about 15 minutes more. Cool slightly, then transfer the mixture to a blender and blend until smooth (be careful—the mixture is still hot). Return the soup to its pot on the stove and turn the heat to medium. In a small bowl, whisk the sour cream to loosen it a little, then slowly add a ladleful of the warm soup to the bowl, stirring to incorporate (this will prevent the sour cream from curdling). Pour the sour cream mixture back into the pot, stirring to combine.

Taste, and season with salt and pepper as needed. Finally, add a squeeze of lemon juice. Taste. Bring the soup back up to a simmer before serving but take care not to boil it or the sour cream may separate.

Serve hot, with a swirl of sour cream on top and a light dusting of cumin.

Beetroot and Parsnip Salad

Beetroot is a superfood. Eat it raw and your immune system will thank you. I use it often—to dip into *bagna càuda*, shaved thin and topped with dollops of *burrata* in summer, and lightly pickled in vegetable salads like this one.

From the roof farm I have added sweet parsnips and the indefatigable dwarf kale. With sappy apples and pungent shallot, this is an instant winter tonic. (An addition of pistachio nuts, pieces of dried apricot, and a side of small toasts topped with warmed fresh goat cheese would transform this from a separate course into the main event.)

≪ SERVES SIX ≫

FOR THE SALAD

2 tablespoons sugar

1 teaspoon salt

¼ cup (60 ml) sherry vinegar

3 medium beets, peeled and sliced into thick matchsticks

3 medium parsnips, peeled and cut crosswise into thin rounds

1 farmers' market apple, cored and very thinly sliced

A handful of baby kale leaves, or large leaves, torn up

FOR THE SHERRY VINAIGRETTE

1 tablespoon sherry vinegar

¼ teaspoon sugar

1 teaspoon mustard

Salt and freshly ground black pepper

4 tablespoons extra-virgin olive oil

1 shallot, minced

Make the salad: In a large bowl, dissolve the sugar and salt in the sherry vinegar and ¼ cup (60 ml) of water. Add the beets and toss to coat. Set aside for an hour to create a quick pickle. Drain the beets and blot them dry on paper towels.

On a pretty serving plate, stack the beets, parsnips, apples, and kale in alternating layers to make a good-looking heap.

Make the vinaigrette: In a small bowl, whisk together the sherry vinegar, sugar, mustard, and salt and pepper to taste, whisking until the sugar is dissolved. Whisk in the oil until emulsified. Add the shallot to the dressing.

Drizzle the salad with the vinaigrette just before serving.

Oxtail Stew

Economical and old-fashioned oxtail makes about the best casserole I can think of. Cooked gently and long, the meat collapses from its bones and the sauce is beautifully enriched by the aromatic vegetables and the bones themselves. Happy guests tend to want to lick their fingers.

⟪ SERVES SIX ⟫

12 medium to large pieces of oxtail (2 for each guest, or the balance in small pieces!)

2 tablespoons brandy

Salt

Freshly ground black pepper

⅓ cup (40 g) flour, for dusting

4 tablespoons (60 ml) olive oil

2 onions, finely chopped

3 cloves garlic, sliced

2 large carrots, chopped small

2 stalks celery, chopped small

8 sprigs thyme

6 sprigs parsley, leaves and stems

2 bay leaves

2 cups (480 ml) red wine

1 cup (240 ml) beef or veal stock

Arrange the oxtails on a large platter. Sprinkle the brandy over them. Season them with salt and pepper. Shake the flour over to coat them lightly and dust off any excess. (The flour helps to thicken their cooking liquid later.) Turn the oxtails and season and flour the other side.

Heat 2 tablespoons of the olive oil in a large Dutch oven over medium-high heat. When it begins to ripple add the oxtails, about four at a time. Brown their tops, bottoms, and sides; remove and repeat until they have all been browned. Transfer to a platter.

If there is still oil left in the pot, sauté the onions, garlic, carrots, and celery over medium heat until the onions are translucent, 6 to 8 minutes. If the oil has disappeared, add the other 2 tablespoons, heat, and then sauté the vegetables. Return the oxtails to the pot with the vegetables, add the thyme, parsley, and bay leaves and pour in the wine. Increase the heat and bring to a boil for a minute, then add the stock and enough water to just cover the tops of the oxtails. Stir well to make sure there is nothing sticking to the bottom of the pot.

Cover and keep at a steady simmer until very tender, about 3 hours. After 90 minutes, remove the lid. Stir occasionally to prevent sticking. Allow to cool, and skim off any fat that has risen to the top. Reheat, and check for seasoning.

Serve directly from the Dutch oven.

Buttermilk Mashed Potatoes

Does one need a recipe for mashed potatoes? Perhaps. The simplest and most luxurious of comfort foods, this has sometimes been my winter supper, in a bowl, nothing more. Served with the oxtail, it provides a soft sponge for the good juices, and a creamy mouthful with the rich sauce. An old-fashioned potato ricer gives the smoothest puree imaginable. A potato masher is no good. Buy a ricer. Now.

SERVES SIX

8 medium-large Yukon Gold potatoes, peeled and cut into quarters

3 tablespoons unsalted butter

¾ cup (180 ml) warm buttermilk

Salt

Freshly ground black pepper

Place the potatoes in a large pot and add water to cover. Salt the water, then bring it to a boil and cook the potatoes until tender, about 15 minutes. Drain into a large colander. Place 1 tablespoon of the butter into the pot in which the potatoes were cooked. Using a potato ricer, push the potatoes back into the warm pot, on top of the butter melting in the bottom. Once all the riced potatoes are in the pot, cut the remaining butter into small pieces and add them to the pot, stirring very well, until they have melted. Add the buttermilk in a thin stream, stirring constantly. Taste. Season very well with salt and pepper. This can be heated very gently, covered, before you need it. Add a little more warm buttermilk if necessary.

Baked Apples

Humankind's millionth error: underrating overbaked apples. Caramelized skin, explosively hot sweet pulp, slightly scorched raisins, a spoon-coating syrup, helped along by the knob of butter tucked where the core should be . . .

My mother fed us baked apples as children, and I have never lost my love for them. This may be a modest dessert but it is deeply satisfying and entirely true to season. A scoop of vanilla ice cream, a lick of cream. Or nothing. Just don't burn your tongue. Sometimes I eat one for lunch.

The apples can be prepared up to a day ahead of time, kept cold, and then roasted an hour before you need them.

⟪ SERVES SIX ⟫

6 apples (Fuji, Jonagold, or Jonathan), cored	⅛ teaspoon ground cloves	3 tablespoons brown sugar	3 tablespoons unsalted butter
¾ cup (110 g) raisins	Pinch of ground allspice	¼ cup (60 ml) fresh lemon juice	Heavy cream, for serving

Preheat the oven to 400°F (200°C).

Slit the apple skins horizontally in two or three places along their circumference. In a small bowl, combine the raisins, cloves, allspice, and sugar. Arrange the apples in a baking dish and stuff each with the raisin mixture, dividing it evenly. Pour the lemon juice over the tops. Add ½ cup (120 ml) water to the dish—this will combine with their cooking juices to form a caramel sauce. Press ½ tablespoon of the butter into each apple, and roast for an hour, until the flesh is soft and richly golden-brown. The baking dish should never dry out—add a little water if it has evaporated.

Serve hot, topped with the caramel sauce from the baking dish, with a jug of cream for pouring over the apples.

MARCH

NEW YORK IN MARCH

Average temperatures: 48°F / 34°F (9°C / 1°C)

March is the month of great upheaval and change.

Unpredictable days are gray and damp then heartbreakingly blue or muffled suddenly by snow. Sap rises above the cold earth and into dark branches. Difficult March lays the groundwork for effusive April, who gets all the credit. Buds are tightly wound with the promise of spring, anticipation in floral form. The botanical clock has started to tick. Loudly.

In Central Park, Siberian squill mirrors the blue of the sky beneath soaring empty trees. Birds appear in The Ramble on exposed tree trunks—a blue nuthatch against the bark as it prospects for insects beginning to stir in the shallow sunlight. An Upper East Sider exercises her bunny on a leash on the green grass. Winter honeysuckle's demure white flowers pump out their powerful lemony scent, the untidy shrub seducing and confusing passersby with its sprawling camouflage.

March begins yellow. The Cornelian cherries flower early, festooned with pollen umbels, the modest trees becoming golden silhouettes. All over the city daffodils start to unfurl, trumpeting sunlight from medians and window boxes. They turn the Brooklyn Botanic Garden's low green hills into England for weeks at a time, transfixing visitors who insinuate themselves among the flowers to pose for pictures. Forsythia, sudden and electric, spills over stone walls, its drab green summer hedge now an impenetrable yellow wall. In woodland thickets in Inwood and Staten Island, where dead leaves still dust the forest floor beneath bare trees, spicebush buds are a yellow constellation in the pale woods. On the floor of Prospect Park's forest, the last in Brooklyn, an early bloodroot flower opens, innocent of the human litter that surrounds it.

Near home, around the corner on Pacific Street in Cobble Hill, the camellia I watch every year opens deep carmine, surprised at itself. As the beautiful flowers drop, someone in that brownstone arranges them on either side of the stoop steps, all the way to the front door. A stairway, perhaps, to heaven. A Dawn viburnum blooms on Warren Street. Its spicy flowers are followed by the first pale spring cherries, the delicate *Prunus subhirtella*, restrained in advance of the showgirl Kanzans in their can-can skirts that romp through the city in late April.

From the flower sellers on Atlantic Avenue I buy weekly bunches of daffodils. Next door, at Mr. Kim's (properly Atlantic Fruit and Vegetable, but we call it Mr. Kim's) I cheat, and buy green asparagus spears from parts south. Local asparagus is a month away.

We still like empty shorelines. On Vincent's birthday, with high cirrus striping the washed sky, we take the subway to the end of the line and then board a bus bound for the Far Rockaways, part of the string of barrier islands that shelters New York from the Atlantic Ocean. Baguette and saucisson are packed, cameras are locked and loaded. Here, beyond the dunes, there is no spring profusion. The beach is austere; the only interruptions to its surface are the shells and smooth stones left by the retreating tide. Mussels cluster around exposed wooden pilings. We spread our *kikoi* on the sand and eat our picnic and sip our cool red wine quietly, finding respite from the cement and streets and traffic in this wide open silence, the collapsing waves, the wheeling seabirds. The sea is silver and blue, the seashore vegetation wind bitten, gray, and reclusive. We ride back into Brooklyn with salt in our hair.

I am impatient to start foraging again, and late in the month Vincent and I ride the A to its most northern stop, at Inwood Hill Park in Manhattan to look for field garlic in the unlittered woods. I find its flavor more intense and sweeter when cooked than that of ramps. Field garlic is ready for pulling earlier in the season, too. Gathering it beneath the old tulip trees and red oaks, with violets and Dutchman's breeches blooming in the dry leaf litter and a suggestion of gauzy leaves overhead, I feel spring fizzing in my blood. We find an artist in the woods, an elderly Korean man who makes wide and swirling circles in the humus, meticulously swept and maintained, and who has trained a woodpecker to eat from his hand. We ride home, our garlic pungent in the subway car, Vince shifting uneasily as his French nose prickles at our own growing presence. New passengers sniff the air speculatively.

Farmers' markets are turning from shades of earth to rainbow palettes of contradiction and temptation. Heaped in crates and baskets are last year's apples and potatoes and root vegetables. Potted plants that have been forced to bright succulence in greenhouses turn the nursery tables into explosions of muscari and hyacinth, violas and pansies, all weeks ahead of the weather's schedule. In what remains of the Flower District, on its 28th Street sidewalks, heavily scented narcissus tilt beside primroses and ranunculus whose petals do not stand a chance against the freezes that still swoop down upon the city with little warning.

But this is New York. If you want it now, you can buy spring early.

Field Garlic Roast Chicken

If I were forced to choose the one dish I like best, it would be roast chicken. Crackly skin, sticky juices, a bed of potatoes. It is open to limitless variation, suggested by the seasons—those without and those within.

≪ SERVES TWO HUNGRY PEOPLE, WITH LEFTOVERS ≫

FOR THE FIELD GARLIC STUFFING

2 strips of bacon, sliced crosswise into ribbons

1 cup (100 g) finely chopped field garlic, white and green parts

1 cup (110 g) bread crumbs

Zest of ¼ lemon

1 tablespoon fresh lemon juice

¼ cup (38 g) crumbled feta cheese

Freshly ground black pepper

Salt

FOR THE CHICKEN AND POTATOES

1 medium chicken, rinsed and patted dry

5 medium potatoes, cut into thin rounds

3 sprigs thyme

Juice of 1 lemon

Salt and freshly ground black pepper

1 cup (240 ml) water or white wine or vermouth

Preheat the oven to 450°F (220°C).

Make the stuffing: In a skillet over medium heat, cook the bacon until its fat is rendered. Add the field garlic and sauté until translucent. Add the bread crumbs, stirring to coat evenly with the bacon fat and garlic. Add the lemon juice and zest. Remove the pan from the heat and stir in the feta. Add pepper to the stuffing and taste for salt.

Make the chicken and potatoes: Gently stuff the chicken. Arrange the sliced potatoes in a roasting pan with the thyme. Season with salt and pepper. Set the chicken on top of the thyme. Squeeze the lemon juice over the chicken, and then season the bird's skin generously with salt and pepper. Add the water or wine to the pan—this forms the basis of the delicious, sticky pan juices.

Put the pan in the oven and do not look at it for an hour. After an hour, check on the liquid and add more water or wine if the pan is dry. After another 15 to 20 minutes, remove the chicken. Let it rest for 10 minutes in the pan before carving. The skin will be perfectly crisp, the meat moist, the juices caramelized, sticky, and slightly tart. Remove the stuffing from the chicken. Carve the bird and arrange the pieces in the pan on the potatoes, with the stuffing served on the side.

THE MARCH TERRACE

Tentative gardening on the little terrace begins. I am longing to touch the soil, to plant, to see movement. At street level, life is rising inside trees and stirring under the ground, and my elevated and cold island becomes the laboratory for a premature gardener's itch.

I consider the fig, carefully. There is nothing I can do about it, but every March I wonder whether I really see faint green at the tips. Has it survived? Or has my root pruning killed it? On the edge of the terrace it receives a full day of sun, from sunrise to sunset, its stiff branches basking in the sunlight and all the promise of figs to come starting to percolate in its hidden veins.

The dull green boxwoods show no obvious signs of life. Leaning in closer, though, I can see that they are forming long, tight buds which, in warmer weather, will turn into a brilliant and tender green ripple of new growth all over their trimmed forms.

Because the terrace is protected, the soil in the pots is usually workable by now and I dig down to see what has become of the lilies. Which ones have rotted in the vicious freeze-thaw cycle, and which have multiplied? I reorganize and replant, getting my hands dirty with the good smell of cold earth. In the gravel at the base of the pots the pale blue violets begin to bloom. This is spring!

The first herb to shows signs of life is the tarragon. Growing in an improbably tiny pot, it sends up soft new shoots smelling faintly of anise when I crush a leaf between my cold fingers. I control myself and allow it to grow another few inches. The chives show sappy, stunted emerald spikes, still trapped in papery white sheaths before bursting free and forming compact mounds. Like a herbivore deprived of my grazing, I stare at them intently. Estorbo's catnip has downy gray leaves crowding compactly around the dead stalks of last year's stems. The tiny seedlings of calamintha have started to emerge. Hundreds. Feeling guilty, I pull them up one by one, knowing that a time must come when their tenacious roots will make weeding a chore. Their piercing minty fresh breath stings the March morning.

I prune the shrub roses hard. While cold weather lingers in the city the roses break dormancy early against their protected, east-facing wall and new red shoots emerge. If the month has been wet and warm, precocious rose-buds form, weeks ahead of roses on the street. A shipment of bare root roses arrives from David Austin—a new Abraham Darby, and a red Munstead Wood. I soak the spindly roots in water and plant them carefully and doubt-fully. They seem bereft of life.

I plant. Hungry for fresh salad leaves, I sow the first crop of the new year's greens on the roof farm and on the terrace edge: mizuna, mustard, wild arugula, winter cress, spicy microgreens. I soak dry peas and fava beans and plant them in big pots, cold weather crops for salads in April. I cover the pots and troughs with chicken wire against the neurotic digging of the roof squir-rels and the unwelcome presence of foreign cats. By month's end the seed-lings have emerged and I thin them, crunching the slender discards greedily. Estorbo, excited about gardening and good smells and fresh shoots, watches me hungrily, chewing any offered greens with whiskery pleasure.

March is my unorthodox month for planting garlic on the roof farm, for a crop harvestable by midsummer. Organic, store-bought heads are separated into cloves and planted an inch below the surface of some nice, fluffy, twelve-inches-deep soil mix, leaving half a hand's breadth between cloves. As I work on the exposed silvertop roof, the Staten Island ferry barks its long departure horn and moves into the thin white mist that hovers over the water of New York Harbor.

Indoors and impatient, I sow trays of summer seeds, greedy for crops to come: bush beans, eggplants, cucumbers, ancho peppers, squash. Tomatoes. Watermelons. One can hope. Outdoors I plant instant pansies. They can withstand a freeze. Their color among the red pots and lifeless perennials seems wonderful.

The promise of the early garden disappears overnight. Sometime in the night the traffic on the street becomes hushed and the small window in the bedroom, open to the cold air, sends in the quilted sound of wheels on snow. Beneath a thick white cover spring seems unavoidably but deliciously detained. I relish this delay in the beginning of the inevitable.

I hear geese in the night. Flying high. I love this fugitive sound of life on the move, of seasons heeded. In daylight I hear them again and rush out to the terrace, look up into the arc of blue, and find them. They are white. Snow geese. Heading north-northwest.

By the end of the month the tender climbing rose leaves have turned bright green and a lily shoot has broken the surface in one of the largest pots on the terrace. It looks crisp and delicious.

Clearly, I am delirious.

Salad Thinnings with Fresh Mozzarella

I can't bear to throw away the long-legged seedlings that I thin from my various sowings of early salad leaves. They are the first succulent green things I have seen in months. I nibble a few on the spot, but then I have to make this ritual dish, every early spring, to prolong my enjoyment of the pale stalks and their monocot leaves. And mozzarella is not just for tomatoes (though by March I am already gritting my teeth to avoid buying the ubqiutous store-red sirens, knowing I have months yet to go . . .).

You can re-create this salad at any other time of year using pea shoots or sprouts in place of leaf thinnings.

« SERVES TWO »

1 tablespoon sugar

½ teaspoon salt

¼ cup (60 ml) sherry vinegar

1 medium beet, peeled and sliced thinly into rounds

1 (9-ounce/260-g) ball buffalo mozzarella, sliced thickly

A handful of salad leaf thinnings, roots sniped off, stems and leaves intact

Excellent extra-virgin olive oil

Freshly ground black pepper

In a small bowl, dissolve the sugar and salt in the vinegar. Add the beet slices. Leave the beets to marinate for 30 minutes, turning them once or twice, for an instant pickle. Drain the brine from the beets.

On two small plates, alternate slices of pickled beet and mozzarella. Top with the salad leaf thinnings. Drizzle some olive oil across the top and finish with a quick grinding of black pepper.

MARCH MENU

March remains very cold, with temperatures plummeting at night. The still-long evenings call for cooking that warms the apartment, something that will seem like a claustrophobic memory, come thick July and August.

Short ribs are a cold-season party staple—a low-fuss, deeply satisfying and economical main course to serve to friends just in from the cold. If you have leftovers, the risotto they make the next day is almost better than the main event. The potato gratin cooks while the ribs are braising. A robust salad is an excellent tonic to counteract the over-anticipation of spring fever, a pairing of bitter with sweet.

While oranges are a deceptively simple end to a meal, the peeled fruit absorbing its bath of rich Cointreau looks as beautiful as it tastes, and the straightforward, familiar flavor is enhanced by the alcohol. And after all that wonderful meat, the oranges' antioxidants have work to do.

Rosé Cocktail

Pink wine seems like a party. The bitterness of the orange oils rubbed onto the sugar cube speak to the dessert of fresh fruit, and create a neat bookend for this menu.

⟪ MAKES ONE DRINK ⟫

1 sugar cube	1 strip of orange peel	Sparkling rosé, chilled

Rub the orange peel against the sugar cube and drop the cube into the bottom of a Champagne flute. Top with sparkling rosé (or Champagne, you reckless devil).

early spring supper

Rosé Cocktail

Radicchio and Raisin Salad

Short Ribs with Field Garlic and Red Wine

Potato Gratin with Cream, Garlic, and Thyme

Oranges Macerated in Cointreau

Radicchio and Raisin Salad

I enjoy bitter flavors as long as there is some relief in sight, and the radicchio is offset perfectly by sweet raisins, crunchy endive, and a hit of warm acid from the white balsamic vinegar. Adding the thinnings from my spicy mesclun salad crop gives a final, peppery crunch.

《 SERVES SIX 》

FOR THE SALAD

1 head round purple radicchio

3 heads treviso (or Belgian endive)

½ cup (120 ml) white balsamic vinegar (or substitute an equal amount white wine vinegar plus 1 tablespoon sugar)

⅓ cup (48 g) golden raisins

FOR THE WHITE BALSAMIC VINAIGRETTE

1 tablespoon white balsamic vinegar

Pinch of salt

Freshly ground black pepper

3 tablespoons walnut oil

TO SERVE

1 cup (55 g) salad leaf thinnings, roots trimmed (substitute hot microgreens or wild arugula)

¼ cup (28 g) toasted pecans, roughly chopped

Make the salad: Peel off the leaves from the head of radicchio and tear into large pieces. Separate the treviso or endive leaves and slice each heart in half lengthwise.

In a small pan over low heat, warm the vinegar until it starts to simmer, and then add the raisins. Poach the raisins very gently over very low heat for 5 minutes. Allow to cool. Remove the raisins from the vinegar and set aside.

Make the vinaigrette: In a large bowl, just before serving, whisk together the vinegar, salt, pepper to taste, and the oil.

Add the radicchio, treviso or endive, and raisins to the bowl with the dressing and toss. Plate on a shallow platter and toss the spicy seedlings or microgreens and nuts over at the last minute (too early and the nuts will absorb the dressing and become soggy, and the tender thinnings will bruise in the vinegar).

Short Ribs with Field Garlic and Red Wine

Short ribs are a very versatile cut of beef, falling off the bone when cooked long and gently, or juicy when sliced rare off a summer grill.

If you don't have field garlic popping out of your lawn or in a nearby wood or field, substitute scallions or ramps. Failing those, small, peeled shallots would be delicious, too.

⧼ SERVES SIX ⧽

6 short ribs, sawn in half so each piece is about 4 inches (10 cm) long, on or off the bone	Salt Freshly ground black pepper	2 cups (200 g) field garlic bulbs and greens (discard the tough stem part)	2 cups (480 ml) red wine 8 juniper berries

Preheat the oven to 350°F (180°C).

Season the short ribs with salt and pepper. Allow to sit for 5 minutes so that some of the juice is drawn out. This will help caramelize the outside of the meat.

Warm a heavy pan over high heat. When it is very hot sear the short ribs, about a minute to a side, until just brown. Do this in batches; do not over-crowd the pan or it will lose too much heat. Remove the short ribs and set aside on a plate.

While you are browning the meat, blanch the field garlic bulbs for a minute in boiling water. Drain and set aside.

Place half the field garlic in the bottom of a roasting pan. Add the short ribs, the rest of the field garlic, the red wine, and juniper berries. Transfer the pan to the oven and cook for 2 hours, tented with foil. Uncover and cook for another 45 minutes, making sure that there is still liquid in the pan. Add water if the pan looks dry.

Serve straight from the pan or from a warmed bowl, scraping up as much juice as possible and spooning it over the ribs.

Potato Gratin with Cream, Garlic, and Thyme

In one of my favorite books, *Bistro Cooking*, Patricia Wells provides ten recipes for potato gratin. I knew I liked the lady. Gratins, like chickens, lend themselves to endless variation, all with satisfying differences in character.

Potatoes are best friends with butter, cream, and milk. A rich gratin is easily a main course in its own right, a cold day lunch, perhaps, served with a green salad. Pairing it with ribs is over the top, but, as my father says, "Life is nothing without excess."

Occasionally.

A rectangular ceramic or enameled baking dish with sides about 3 inches (7.5 cm) high is perfect. A heavy frying pan works just as well.

⟨⟨ SERVES SIX ⟩⟩

8 medium-large potatoes, peeled	¼ cup (60 ml) cream	6 sprigs fresh thyme, leaves pulled from stems	4 cloves garlic, sliced paper thin
2 ½ cups (600 ml) milk	2 tablespoons unsalted butter		Salt and freshly ground black pepper

Preheat the oven to 350°F (180°C).

Slice the potatoes very thin. Combine the milk and cream in a separate bowl.

Grease the baking dish generously with 1 tablespoon of the butter. Cover the bottom of the pan with a layer of overlapping potato slices. Sprinkle them with some thyme leaves and garlic slices, and season with salt and pepper. Repeat with layers of potatoes and more thyme, garlic slices, and salt and pepper until you have almost reached the top of the dish. Leave about ½ inch (12 mm) free to accommodate bubbling liquids (which could spill over and cause a terrible stink in the oven—ask me how I know). Pour the milk and cream mixture carefully over the potatoes. The liquid should just reach the uppermost potato layer. If it does not, add some additional milk or water. Dot little flecks of the remaining tablespoon of butter over the top.

Bake for 90–120 minutes, cooking the potatoes to creaminess with a brown top. Serve at the table directly from the baking dish.

Oranges Macerated in Cointreau

Oranges are in peak season, and the ubiquitous and taken-for-granted citrus fruit becomes sophisticated when peeled of all pith, sliced, and chilled thoroughly in a shallow bath of Cointreau and sugar. It is a light, easy dessert. Candied orange zest adds another layer of pleasure.

If you are Cointreau-deprived, good brandy, tequila, or Cognac work well.

≪ SERVES SIX ≫

6 medium oranges	½ cup (100 g) sugar	1 tablespoon brown sugar	¼ cup (60 ml) Cointreau

Peel the orange zest from 2 oranges in strips as long as you can manage, cutting from the top to the bottom of the orange to keep the strips as straight as possible. Reserve the peeled oranges. Cut each strip of zest lengthwise into slivers. Bring a small saucepan of water to a boil and blanch the strips of zest for 1 minute. Pour off the water and return the zest to the saucepan with the sugar and 1 cup (240 ml) water. Bring to a boil, stirring to dissolve the sugar, then reduce the heat and cook at a low simmer until tender and syrupy, about 25 minutes.

Remove any remaining pith from the reserved peeled oranges.

Peel the remaining 4 oranges, discarding the peels and pith.

Slice the peeled oranges fairly thinly crosswise. Take out any pips with the point of a knife. Arrange the sliced oranges in a pretty, shallow serving bowl or plate. Sprinkle the sugar over the fruit and pour the Cointreau over all the slices. Refrigerate, covered, for at least 4 hours, spooning the juices back over the fruit several times. Top the cold orange slices with candied orange zest and some of the sticky, slightly bitter syrup leftover from candying.

APRIL

NEW YORK IN APRIL

April is what the cold world has been waiting for.

We range far and wide, riding all the way to the ends of every subway line. And then we take the bus—for the love of open spaces, flowers, and things green (and often edible). Everywhere, we are flanked by the white callery pear blossom that is synonymous with April on New York's streets.

In Pelham Bay in the Bronx we walk in the forest near the water and the rocky islands of the Long Island Sound and find drifts of tiny white flowers under the trees in the fallen leaves. They are cutleaf toothwort, an increasingly rare native wildflower. Nearby is a pocket of anemones on stems like threads. The ranunculus cups of invasive lesser celandine are a brilliant yellow beside the path. In this forest, still rustling with winter's leaves, there are few people to be seen, other than a clump of birdwatchers with mammoth lenses waiting for a greater horned owlet to raise its fluffy head from a shattered stump that rises twenty feet above the floor of the greening woods. We picnic on bread and paté on a rocky outcrop, sipping our air-chilled sauvignon blanc. On the walk back I stop to kneel beneath the tall hollow canes of last year's Japanese knotweed and cut big bunches of the new, succulent shoots that sprout from each cluster near the beach. The fragile white candy-striped flowers of spring beauty crowd the grass near our bus stop.

At the opposite end of the city, in the Brooklyn Botanic Garden, I make an annual pilgrimage to see the gentle unfolding of the cloaks that wrap each bloodroot stem in the Native Garden. It is a drama in miniature. Every small white flower blooms alone, wrapped in modesty. Later, the leaves of trout lilies here and in Central Park's Ramble form spotted mats beneath fragile stalks supporting the fulvous flowers. These ephemerals belong to a delicate, indigenous spring, still surprisingly alive—though under great pressure—in wilder parks and careful gardens. They disappear as the forest leafs out and its shade sends them back into the warming earth.

I cross the road and wander in the woods of Prospect Park, finding, off the path and among the weedy garlic mustard flowers, carpets of blue violets, entirely hidden from passersby. Unable to restrain myself, I gather a posy. The last time I held such a fragrant bunch was after picking deep purple violets from under the lilac tree in my mother's garden, on Paul Roux Street in Bloemfontein. The feeling is no different. I wrap their slender stems carefully in a leaf and they ride home with me on the subway, lasting for days in the apartment and thrilling me every time I see them.

At Dead Horse Bay we scout the sand for old glass bottles. This was a garbage dump until the middle of the last century and yields attractive treasure as the bay's tides eat the landfill away. On land, white beach plum blossom is like foam on its tangled branches and autumn olive saturates the sea air with scent. We turn to the grassy pathways to scout for pokeweed and find its supple young stems perfect for cutting. Wild lettuce grows in tender emerald clumps. There are common milkweed shoots, too, and we bring home the ingredients for a slew of new dishes after picnicking on the grass.

Surrounding these quiet woodland and shoreline lives, the roar of an imported spring grows. Magnolias, their limbs heavy with waxy blooms, lead the way—Ava Gardners to the Audrey Hepburns and Brigitte Bardots of the woods and water. Confettied cherry blossoms, early and late, pale and flushed, erupt before and after the magnolias' profusion. Parks that have been empty and contemplative for months seethe with people luxuriating beneath pink Kanzan canopies—beside the reservoir in Central Park and on the Cherry Esplanade at the Brooklyn Botanic Garden where voluptuous peonies hold court next door. On Carroll Street, one neighborhood downstream of Cobble Hill, the frilled petals of the cherries turn a brownstone corner at sundown to glowing rose. In Boerum Hill, and all the Villages, bunches of wisteria drip from fire escapes and townhouses.

My mother comes to visit from Cape Town. She would like to see New York in spring. I take her to the farmers' market at Union Square, where mounds of electric microgreens, foraged nettles, and yellow flowers from winter's brassicas nestle beside the first bouquets of ramps—white, garnet, and green and tied with twine. Spears of early asparagus are stacked in bunches, crates high. Local lilac, ranunculus, and red and purple and cerise anemones create bottlenecks of shoppers hungry for real flowers.

We visit the Conservatory Gardens in the northeast corner of Central Park, where there is as much spring within easy reach as it is possible to fit. Massed collections of yellow and cream daffodils ricochet off blue, musky-scented grape hyacinths. Around them the more subtle yellows and greens of native plantings wrap the hedged formal garden. The hedge itself is in bloom and loud with bees browsing the ilex flowers. The famous circle of tulips around the bronze fountain is lilac and purple with splashes of fuchsia and yellow. After a picnic of farmers' market asparagus and mayonnaise,

prosciutto, and a hidden bottle of New Zealand sauvignon blanc, eaten and sipped in a cathedral of old crab apple trees in full bloom, my mother, the gardener, says decidedly: This is one of the wonders of the world.

And it is. All we can see is blossom. Branches meet above us to reveal one scrap of cobalt sky. Petals drift to the flagstones at our feet. The air is filled with the icy spice of crab apple. All we can hear is the ascending peep of a migrating songbird's call in the flowers that obscure the world beyond us.

Forager's Special

Japanese Knotweed Soup

When cooked in moist heat, knotweed collapses into a lemony creaminess reminiscent of sorrel. I use it in slow-cooked curries, beneath chickens, and add it to lamb shank pot roasts.

Pick fat, juicy shoots up to about 16 inches (40 cm) tall. Knotweed is high in oxalic acid, so avoid it if you have kidney problems. If you have no knotweed, substitute 4 cups (220 g) of shredded, loosely packed sorrel.

❮❮ SERVES FOUR ❯❯

1 tablespoon unsalted butter

½ cup (80 g) finely chopped shallots

4 cups (about 340 g) skinned and sliced knotweed, joints discarded

2 small potatoes, peeled and thinly sliced

4 cups (1 L) hot chicken or vegetable stock

Salt

Freshly ground black pepper

Heavy cream, for serving (optional)

In a pot, melt the butter until it foams. Add the shallots and cook gently until they are translucent. Add the knotweed and cook, stirring, for 2 to 3 minutes until the color of the knotweed changes from fresh green to drab khaki. Add the potatoes and the stock and cook until the potato slices are tender, about 10 minutes. Allow the mixture to cool, then puree it in batches in a blender. Strain each batch through a fine-mesh sieve into a bowl. Return the soup to the stove and heat until simmering, then season to taste. A swirl of cream before serving is never a bad idea.

Fruit Buns

Spiced fruit buns are a year-round supermarket staple in South Africa, a rare happy colonial hangover. Months before Easter the buns suddenly become Hot Cross Buns.

≪ MAKES 12 TO 16 BUNS ≫

FOR THE YEAST MIXTURE

⅔ cup (160 ml) milk

1 tablespoon yeast

1 teaspoon sugar

FOR THE DOUGH

1 pound (450 g) flour

½ teaspoon cinnamon

¼ teaspoon allspice

¼ teaspoon nutmeg

¼ teaspoon cloves

4 ounces (100 g) butter

3 tablespoons superfine sugar

¼ teaspoon salt

2 eggs, whisked

FOR THE FRUIT

5 ½ ounces (150 g) raisins or currants

2 ounces (50 g) candied citrus peel, chopped small

FOR THE EGG GLAZE

1 egg

3 tablespoons milk

FOR THE CROSS

3 tablespoons flour

Pinch salt

1 tablespoon sugar

FOR THE SUGAR GLAZE

1 tablespoon sugar

Heat the milk in a pan until tepid. Stir in the yeast and sugar and allow it to proof.

Put the flour in a large mixing bowl and grate the butter into it. Rub the butter and flour together with your fingertips until it resembles coarse sand. Add the sugar and salt.

Add the eggs to the flour with the milk and yeast mixture. This will make a loose dough. Turn the dough out onto a floured work surface and knead for 10 minutes, until smooth and supple. Grease a large bowl, place the dough inside, and cover. Set the dough aside until it has doubled in size—1 to 3 hours.

Remove the dough to a floured work surface, flatten it out a little, and scatter some of the raisins and candied citrus peel across it. Knead again to spread the fruit around evenly. Do this in stages.

Divide the dough into 12 to 16 equal pieces and form them into round shapes. Put on a greased baking sheet, leaving an inch (2.5 cm) between them for rising. If you are making crosses, lightly score a cross into the top of each bun using a sharp knife.

Cover the buns and let rise until doubled in size.

Preheat the oven to 400°F (200°C).

Make the egg glaze: Beat together the egg and milk. Brush this over the buns and put them in the hot oven now if you are not making crosses.

Make the crosses: Mix the flour and salt with enough cold water to make a slightly runny paste. Paint the top of each bun with egg glaze as above, and then, using a piping bag or a teaspoon, fill in the score marks with the paste.

Put the buns into the oven and bake for about 25 minutes, until the buns are golden and sound hollow when tapped.

Make the sugar glaze: In a small bowl, mix the sugar with 1 tablespoon of water. Brush the buns with the sugar glaze while piping hot, then transfer them to a rack to cool.

THE APRIL TERRACE

Suddenly in April, a robin starts to sing. The song is improbably bucolic, lovely in the enormous city. Listening to it, I feel as if I have been holding my breath and am now able to exhale for the first time in months. In the following days, near 5 A.M., the robin is joined by others. They are the Brooklyn dawn chorus, returned from winter quarters.

I am busy: watching things grow. The Etoile Violette and the autumn clematis are launching perfectly vertical shoots, pale red and weaving, vulnerable in their search for support. Bee's Jubilee opens into loud pink stripes. Roses leaf out, lilies are rising—sappy green skyscrapers under construction. The wisteria is in bud and in a shady corner foamflower . . . foams. On the gravel floor violets continue to open, delicately and painfully blue. The mint begins to reveal textured leaves which crowd around the bases of the terra-cotta pots. Tiny seedlings erupt in corners of the terrace floor and I wait to see their secondary and identifying leaves before pulling them out. I don't know what they are yet. They may be useful. I feel like a hoarder.

Each pot on the edge has turned from a drab repository of sticks into a neat pool of green, a circle of dark earth still visible around its edges. In among the herbs, the chives are in bud, making it hard to cut the leaves for fear of severing future flowers. Undeterred, I snip and strew the first chives of the year over a celebratory boiled egg. The catnip begins to bloom in earnest. The fig tree's early leaves are fragile and transparent in the sunlight. The first of the breba crop has emerged from the gray winter branches. I expect it to drop as it always does, but perhaps one will survive to give me an early summer fruit. The Iceberg roses above the doorway spill downward in their first pink-tinged flush. Alpine strawberries are like green water drops at the tips of their arched stems.

The trays of warm-weather seedlings destined for the roof farm graduate from the floor of the apartment to the stone table, where they enjoy days of sunshine. They resemble real vegetables and I resist the urge to plant them out on the exposed roof, waiting for the last average frost date to pass, watching the weather reports suspiciously. At the hint of a dip into the 40s, or a heavy rain shower, I rush them under the outside table and drape its exposed sides with *kikois*. Vincent, under whose dining chair the seedlings have already lived for two weeks, eyes me warily.

And so do the slugs and snails: I wander sleepily onto the terrace one morning with a cup of strong coffee and study the new growth placidly. Then I freeze. A lily shoot has disappeared. A whole shoot, an entire head of flowers, gone. War. Hell. And death! One snail, stupidly attached to the ruined shoot, becomes airborne and floats through the air with the greatest of ease, full of summer lilies in its minute digestive system. That night I set beer traps. By the following morning they are full.

The vengeance of a gardener is no small thing. We are armed to the teeth. With cutting implements and alcohol.

On an unusually warm day, we taste the threat of summer in its stickiness. The crab apple in front of the building has opened and its petals are falling. Up here they smell like fresh water, like hail coming, like snow, faraway, on mountains. I sip my first Kir of the terrace year—my antidote to the terrible hope of spring. Danielle, our neighbor, is perched precariously on her roof in a short skirt, tying up her rose. She caught the gardening bug from me. I throw twine over to her. It is an evening for living outdoors.

I carry my drink up to the roof and collect the paper bag that I have tossed up ahead of my ascent: sprouting potatoes for planting, seeds, a trowel, and a knife. I collect the first fat fava bean leaves and curling pea shoots for a succulent spring salad. The blueberry has opened tiny bell flowers, pale against the young red foliage. The white currant is in lime bloom.

A couple of weeks later the terrace recovers from my promiscuous summer bulb planting chaos: Abyssinian gladiolus, tuberoses, and gloriosa lilies, the results of late-night online shopping. The last two are hopeful experiments. I tuck them into already-stuffed pots and say a horticultural prayer. I pick small pansies from the terrace and arrange them in an egg cup. They are followed by a succession of ranunculus and daffodils, violets, and a minute posy of lesser celandine.

Now the moon rises just south of the ailanthus tree on the next block—almost dead east. It is an opal in the evening sky. In silhouette, the clematis stems head straight toward the first stars.

In the renewed excitement of growth I know that I am experiencing what I can barely remember by late August: an insatiable appetite for fresh greens and flowers, for young flavors and new plants; an appetite that moves me to carry those seed trays indoors and out every day, onto the table and under it, trailing morsels of compost and shredded bark.

The change of season allows us to forget, and in forgetting, we begin again.

Boiled Egg with the First Chives

It may seem peculiar to provide a recipe for a boiled egg. But there is a reason that day-fresh eggs appear on the menu of the acclaimed restaurant Blue Hill at Stone Barns, the model farm in Westchester, New York. Eggs are a perfect food—mellow, soft, and buttery in the mouth. And they don't lie—they tell you where they came from.

A boiled egg is the perfect partner for the first taste of the year's chives, which, when snipped, drip with a fresh, allium-scented sap. These are the first greens of the springing year.

Choose your egg with care. If you are lucky enough to have your own hens, you will be in a small pocket of culinary heaven. Otherwise, find organic or genuinely free-range eggs from a reputable source. The lightly cooked bright yellow yolk, dab of melting butter, sprinkling of chives, and dash of salt and freshly ground black pepper mingle to make one of the best-tasting mouthfuls you could ever possibly enjoy.

Best accompanied with good coffee or excellent tea.

⟨⟨ SERVES ONE ⟩⟩

1 egg

Salt and freshly ground black pepper

1 teaspoon sweet, unsalted butter

A small handful of early chives, snipped

Place the egg in a very small saucepan with enough cold water to cover. Bring to a boil over high heat. Keep at a gentle boil for 3 minutes for an egg with a white that is cooked through and a yolk that is just beginning to set.

Remove the egg from the water with a slotted spoon and place it in an egg cup.

Make a little heap of salt and pepper, mixed together, on a saucer and place the egg cup on the saucer. Slice the cap off the top of the egg. Top the egg with a dab of butter, a pinch of the mixed salt and pepper, and a sprinkling of chives.

Dip in your spoon, and begin. Repeat the seasoning as you delve deeper into the egg.

At markets the brown and buff cold-month crops still say quietly, Eat me. But we are impatient for green, and especially for ramps, the native wild onion that is the food lover's starting pistol to the new season. Late in the month the ramps and other wild and domestic greens start to transform the market tables. And from the roof above our heads I have picked the first fava bean leaves and pea shoots.

We had roast lamb on Sundays, *braaied* lamb chops and ribs, and my mother's Lamb with a Spoon, cooked for a day, is famous. We called it Spam with a Loon. In the States, lamb is pricey, and the leg is reserved for special occasions.

Quebecita

When Mexico and Canada meet in a glass . . .

One April evening, wanting a cocktail to drink on the roof, I found our limited drinks tray stocked only with a very good bottle of aged Chinaco tequila, but no Cointreau, so no margarita was possible. What I did have was a bucket load of maple syrup, thanks to Germaine Versailles, my Quebecois mother-in-law who takes it up intravenously and who believes that everyone else should, too. And I always, always have lemons.

« MAKES ONE DRINK »

3 ounces (6 tablespoons) good tequila	1½ ounces (3 tablespoons) fresh lemon juice	½ ounce (1 tablespoon) maple syrup

Shake this all up vigorously with lots of ice. Strain and pour into a coupe. It will be deep golden and match the twilight.

lamb supper

Quebecita

Fava Bean Leaf and Pea Shoot Salad

Lamb Roasted with Ramps and Anchovies

Apple and Rhine Riesling Soup

Fava Bean Leaf and Pea Shoot Salad

Fat, sweet fava bean and pea leaves, planted in March, are ready for eating by April.

When I started to grow fava beans (also known as broad beans), I was thinking of harvesting the mature bean pods, which I love. But I started to nibble the tender shoots, since they are one of the earliest-maturing and most prolific of leaves growing up on the roof, and I was hungry for any fresh, growing thing. To my delight, the leaves on the growing tips were soft, flavorsome, and gave lettuce more than a run for its money. That first bean crop was never allowed to produce beans. I ate it all. Now I reserve some plants for leaves and others for flowers and pods.

And it was Chinatown that taught me about pea shoots. They overflow from crates on the sidewalk, and are the filling of my favorite dumplings at Dim Sum Go Go. Their raw flavor is sweet—just like the mature peas.

Favas and peas love cold weather, so they start and end my edible growing year.

≪ SERVES FOUR ≫

FOR THE LEMON VINAIGRETTE

1 tablespoon fresh lemon juice

1 tablespoon cream

Pinch of salt

Pinch of sugar

2 tablespoons extra-virgin olive oil

5 cups (275 g) loosely packed, mixed fava bean and pea leaves, tender tips only

Make the vinaigrette: Shake the lemon juice, cream, salt, and sugar in a jar or whisk in a bowl until the sugar and salt have dissolved. Whisk in the oil until emulsified.

Toss the greens with the dressing at the very last minute, and plate.

Lamb Roasted with Ramps and Anchovies

This lamb starts life as a humid pot roast, transforming halfway through cooking to a regular roast. The anchovies that are spiked into the meat dissolve into rich brininess, eventually combining with the red wine and sweet ramps sizzling in the bottom of the pan to make a wonderful juice. While the lamb is resting, slices of bread are fried lightly in a skillet and then rubbed with a raw ramp bulb. Served alongside the meat, they absorb its sauce, while their crisp crusts provide a fragrant crunch with each juicy mouthful.

《 SERVES FOUR 》

2 bunches of ramps (about 20 ramps)

6 anchovy fillets

1 leg of lamb (about 6 pounds / 2.7 kg)

Salt

Freshly ground black pepper

2 cups (480 ml) red wine

12 slices of baguette or 6 slices of a loaf, halved into triangles

½ cup (120 ml) olive oil, for frying

Preheat the oven to 400°F (200°C).

Cut the bulbs of about 6 ramps into thin slivers. Cut each anchovy in half. Using a very sharp, small knife, cut 1-inch-deep (2.5-cm) slits in the top and sides of the lamb in a dozen places. Stuff half an anchovy and a couple of ramp slivers into each slit, using the knife point to push them in. Place the lamb in a roasting pan, season with salt and pepper, and pour the red wine into the pan. Arrange all but one of the remaining ramps around the lamb. Cover with a lid or loosely tent with foil and place in the oven. After an hour, remove the lid or foil tent. Continue roasting for 1 hour more. If the pan shows any sign of drying out, add some water (a high-frequency sizzle from the oven is my clue that more liquid is needed).

Remove the lamb from the oven and leave in its dish to rest for 15 minutes. While the leg is resting, heat ¼ cup (60 ml) of the olive oil in a sauté pan over medium heat. Fry the baguette or bread in two batches, using the remaining ¼ cup (60 ml) oil for the second batch, until the bread is pale golden. Rub each hot slice of bread with the bulb of the remaining raw ramp. Wrap the bread in a large napkin and set aside on a plate to keep warm.

Transfer the rested lamb to a warm serving platter along with the ramps. Pour the pan juices into a small saucepan over medium-high heat until warmed, then decant the liquid into a small heatproof jug or pitcher for serving at the table.

Serve slices of the lamb with bread and ramps alongside and a generous drizzle of juice.

Apple and Rhine Riesling Soup

It is too early for strawberries. Even local rhubarb has not made an appearance. Farmers still need to sell those apples. This clear sweet soup is an unusual way to enjoy them. It was inspired by an extraordinary ice cider vinegar made by Fabrice Lafon in Quebec, from apples that had frozen on the tree (see Note). It is expensive and rich and is to be eaten slowly by the teaspoonful.

The resulting soup is surprising, delicate and light, and entirely seasonal.

Although we love this as an unorthodox cold starter, like the fruit soups of Eastern Europe, it can also be a dessert. Just decrease the acid component.

Note: This vinegar is not widely available, so a good apple cider vinegar can be substituted, with the addition of ½ teaspoon brown sugar per tablespoon.

⟨⟨ SERVES FOUR ⟩⟩

1 bottle dry riesling 1 vanilla bean, slit down its length	1 sweet and fragrant apple, cored, peeled, thinly sliced, and tossed with fresh lemon juice	6 tablespoons (85 g) brown sugar	2 tablespoons ice cider vinegar (see Note)

Bring the wine, 2 cups (480 ml) of water, and the vanilla bean to a simmer and cook to reduce by one quarter. Scrape the vanilla seeds from the softened pod and whisk them into the liquid to break up any clumps. Add the apple and sugar, stirring to dissolve the sugar. Simmer until the apple is tender. Add the vinegar. Taste. The result should be lightly sweet and fragrant with a tart balance. If necessary, add a little more sugar. Ladle the hot soup into warmed shallow bowls with a few apple slices in each.

MAY

In my youngest years my storybooks were filled with talking animals and idealized European countrysides, complete with hedgerows and primroses, but it took the Brooklyn Botanic Garden to show me bluebells. Beneath giant elms whose green shade intensifies the miraculous May blue, the bluebells are like a sky fallen, sleeping in the green. It seems impossible that this unlikely paradise lies between the unromantic arteries of Flatbush Avenue and Eastern Parkway. Yet it does, suspended in disbelief.

Early in the month I walk through Brooklyn Heights to the Promenade, at the end of Remsen Street. I sense the scent of Dutch irises before their lavender forms take shape in the dusk. Here is a real garden behind a low wrought-iron fence, where someone takes bearded irises seriously. Their perfume is a rarely considered garden pleasure. Twenty feet of flowers in the gray light belie the proximity of the hidden and vibrating two-layer, six-lane Brooklyn-Queens Expressway hidden just yards away and below. A few weeks later, roses will have opened in among the fading irises.

On Congress Street a week later the air feels different. There are unfamiliar shadows on the bluestone sidewalk. It is the presence of layers and layers of leaves. The tall trees that line every block have turned from a collection of separate branches traced in tentative lime to a thick and unified green canopy, each crown meeting the next to create the pools of shade we have not known or needed since last summer. Oaks, plane trees, maples, lindens, and callery pears blur their early spring and winter distinctions. Leaves brushing each other in the wind add a new sound to the living layer of the city's grid.

Roses are everywhere. On Union Street beside the stagnant and oil-streaked Gowanus Canal they bloom red in a sidewalk garden—a backdrop for yellow loosestrife and indigo salvia. At the Brooklyn Botanic Garden the view from an overlook down to the Cranford Rose Garden is curiously ageless, the white gazebo, the soft green grass in rows between beds, the wire arches with clematis just beginning to bloom and the collections of roses, old and new, shrub and rambler, single, double, cupped, or flat as saucers. Up close the variety is endless and the scent is rich, even at midday under a paling and warm sky. Visitors press their noses repeatedly into the hearts of flowers and inhale. Sarah Owens, the rosarian, walks up and down, watchful, with her Felcos holstered on her hip, and pollinators buzz among the perennials and annual borders she has planted nearby to bring back healthy insect life.

At the farmers' market at Borough Hall I pounce on the first real strawberries. Under the market's white awnings, small plump berries from New Jersey are heaped into pale blue cardboard boxes, row upon row. The air above them is thick, saturated with the aroma of the first fruit of the new year. It has been a long, long wait. At home I eat the first two layers straight out of the box, without thinking, standing at the kitchen counter and swallowing the warm fruit whole. Our evening drink is a heresy of light red wine, ice, and the sweet, sliced strawberries. It tastes superb.

Late in the month Vincent escorts me to Staten Island. He has experienced a sea change about the most dismissed of New York City boroughs. His first photographic trip here involved becoming stuck in thick mud that he scraped off his legs with useful leaves that turned out to be poison sumac. He never forgot that. Neither did I. Then he discovered—on Google Maps, the way we often find green places to explore in the city—a series of parks near the southern end of the island, and was intrigued. We catch the orange ferry across the harbor, and I set foot on the Staten Island subway for the first time in twelve years of New York life. It travels above ground!

Two stops short of the end of the line, we walk through a suburban neighborhood thick with trees and rampant Japanese knotweed, now shoulder-height. Washing hangs on lines above tall, uncut grass. We cross a busy road and then we are in the woods of Mount Loretto. Leaf humus is soft and damp beneath our feet. Recent rain has produced crops of puffballs in heaps of woodchips. The first striped mosquitoes of the season hover and we break out our South African bug repellant and apply war paint. Leaving the sea-green woods, we walk through fields of grasses edged by tall trees and a church steeple on the horizon. Naturalized and invasive *Rosa multiflora* turns the landscape into an undulating series of confettied hedges. Native wild roses (*Rosa virginiana*), single, pink, and reticent, scramble amongst the weeds. A brown rabbit watches us, unafraid. An osprey sails overhead with a fish in its talons. We reach a beach and see a massive tanker pass in the channel, bound for the open ocean. Here, at the high-tide mark, I find a new flower in bloom, belonging to a shrub I do not know. It turns out to be leadplant, and is beautiful, even before I know its name. Turning back toward the woods, we pass dense colonies of common milkweed, all in bud, so many that I am able to gather a bagful without feeling guilty at depriving a monarch butterfly of a place to lay her eggs. Another small brown rabbit nibbles the grass nearby.

In this state park in a city of 8.3 million people, we have passed just five other humans on Memorial Day weekend, on the cusp of summer.

Milkweed Buds with Ginger and Soy Sauce

Common milkweed buds are a wonderful vegetable. They taste like a cross between tender broccoli and green beans, but it is an unfair comparison, as their flavor is unique. Pick them when the buds are tightly closed, and include at least 4 inches (10 cm) of the tender stalk, too, which is perfectly edible when young. The white latex from the cut stem flows freely and is very sticky. Take care not to collect any larvae of ladybugs, which favor the plants as nurseries.

At home, remove all but the topmost leaves. Submerge the stems and buds in a deep basin of salted water. If there are any hidden insects, they will emerge, swearing.

As a light meal with or without some brown rice, or as a side dish, this is memorably good.

≪ SERVES ONE OR TWO ≫

12 milkweed buds with stems

Salt

1 tablespoon coconut or unscented oil

½ thumb-size piece of ginger, peeled and very thinly sliced into matchsticks

1 tablespoon soy sauce

1 tablespoon fresh lemon juice

¼ teaspoon sugar

Freshly ground black pepper

In a saucepan, bring enough salted water to a boil to cover the milkweed. Blanch the buds and stems for a minute to dispel the latex. Drain and refresh under cold water and pat dry very, very well with a dishcloth or paper towels—the buds tend to absorb a lot of water.

In a saucepan over medium heat, heat the oil. Add the ginger and sauté gently for a few minutes until cooked through. Increase the heat and add the soy sauce, lemon juice, and sugar, stirring briskly to dissolve the sugar. Add the blanched milkweed. Toss several times to heat through and coat with the glaze, and season with pepper. Serve immediately.

THE MAY TERRACE

In these longer, softer days stems have grown tall, so that when I look out at the terrace I see leaves, bending in the slight, warm ruffle of mid-May. Pale strawberries have replaced their white flowers in the collection of pots on the edge. Their serrated foliage is becoming extravagant, no longer the hunched rosettes of early spring. Within a week the fruit is plump and pure crimson.

The catnip flowers are two shades deeper than the sky. Lilac chive buds are opening. I continue with my spring breakfast ritual—boiled eggs with the juicy chives snipped into their hearts.

I plant out my tiny purple basil seedlings, arranging their small pots where the flush of dark leaves will contrast with the calamintha of summer. Three breba figs look as though they may ripen on the tree, giving me a taste of the main crop to come, which will form on new, green growth. The breeze curls over the roof from the harbor and the fig's branches vibrate. A white eddy of rose petals swirls to the gravel.

This is the month of roses. They are my first, and will be my last, flower love. My mother had a rose garden in Bloemfontein where each shrub grew in its own square cut-out of earth in the clipped grass that formed the rows of paths. They were stiff hybrid teas with perfect blooms and rich scent. My small hands handled their first pair of sharp Felcos in that garden, cutting their stems (and my thumb, too, bright child's blood) with its fierce blades. In Brooklyn my own roses climb from two big pots in opposite corners of the terrace, meeting halfway above the sliding door in a drift of white and shell pink. The Iceberg arrived by mail from Texas years ago and covers a wall, partially hiding the air conditioner, and always trying to escape toward our northern neighbor across the rough silvertop in between. The New Dawn was a five-foot pink teepee, a floral ice cream cone, when I bought it from a Long Island nursery. It blooms abundantly but briefly in small tender knots, with a light second flush. I never fail to speculate coldly whether the months of waiting are worth it. These two weeks arrive, and I forgive it everything—the sharp prolific thorns, the lanky growth, the insignificant rebloom.

The climbers are the first to flower and I am acutely aware that I wait all year for these full-blown days of rose blossom. I watch them open almost sadly, knowing how brief, but very sweet, this will be. After midnight I hear the petals of the New Dawn drop in muffled clusters to the terrace floor, entire flowers letting go and falling at once. It is a rare sound, beautiful and final. Sometimes I gather the petals and toss them four floors down, to float to the street, a ghostly petal parade in the dark. A girl walks home alone from a night out, high heels clicking on bluestone sidewalk. I want to hear her laugh as she looks up, and sees them fluttering down, silken confetti.

After a day of gray rain out of the south and turning west—the northern effects of the season's first tropical storm off the Carolinas—the shining gravel floor is carpeted in bruised petals. When the weather clears I will begin deadheading.

The English shrub roses are less fraught, chosen for their ability to rebloom until frost. Living in the sun on the terrace edge, their cut flowers, cupped and fragrant, fill old dairy bottles collected from our forays to Dead Horse Bay. This is luxury, these peony-like flowers of rich apricot and pale pink, a transportable pleasure, small and impermanent Dutch Masters. Abraham Darby's extravagant petals arch over Henry Street. Red Munstead Wood, whose depths tend toward black, inspires me to go in search of deep purple heliotrope for night scent on the coming summer terrace. In Cape Town, when we visit, we smell the heliotrope shrub planted outside my bedroom window all night long. Here, it will be a small annual.

The clematis is completing its sprawling, purple ascent to the top of the Iceberg rose and is a cloud of petals late in the month. Etoile Violette is a generous plant, reviving from the dry sticks that I cut back hard in winter, and is now a vertical and billowing presence in the small space.

On one of the first long, sunlit evenings we picnic on the roof, cirrus clouds diffuse under a sky made wider by vapor trails crossing and feathering the stratosphere. A blue jay skims the silvertop, performing split-second evasive maneuvers—surprised by the two humans who disrupt his mapped topography. We sip our wine and wave at our neighbor Nora Rawlinson on her roof to the west, above Congress Street, where she snips at the wisteria on her pergola. She holds up her cat, Coco, who is leashed, to wave at Estorbo. The network of rooftops declines the conformity of the streets below, sight lines skipping houses and bridging gulfs in between. We are a diminished and elevated population in the golden light. Chimney swifts dart above us in pursuit of insects, their twittering high and sweet.

In the pots on the silvertop the nasturtiums have made green umbrellas, white currants are incomplete strings of hard pearls, volunteer lamb's quarters are ready to eat, and the small tomato seedlings and cucumbers have been planted out. Green garlic is a foot tall; squash leaves grow rounder overnight. The trout lettuce has spots. I sow more of these beautiful leaves at the tomatoes' feet—they will welcome the later shade in summer. The rose that I moved to the roof to recuperate is in full bloom.

The air is soft, and my hair curls for the first time in the year. Up here there is a feeling of weightlessness. We can breathe. The copper domes of Ellis Island across the water look like a silhouetted Kremlin, and Jersey is a distant frontier in receding layers of sunset rose and smoke. Below us on the terrace the *braai* fire is smoldering. When its coals begin to glow we move downstairs again to grill our supper. At the stone table we eat with the fire pleasantly warm at my back, the scent of the roses falling around us.

Our outdoor life has begun. The sun drops, and the light with it. In the first gray of evening the robin's oscillating song begins again from the old television antenna on the roof across the road.

Summer is coming.

Vichyssoise

This delectable soup is liquid comfort. Born and bred in New York, it is the most appropriate thing to sip on the silvertop as we watch the busy New York world go by, on the water and in the sky.

Chopped chives are a mandatory garnish.

≪ SERVES FOUR ≫

6 to 8 leeks

2 tablespoons olive oil

3 medium potatoes, peeled and sliced ¼ inch (6 mm) thick

4 cups (1 L) hot vegetable or chicken stock

Salt and freshly ground black pepper

⅔ cup (160 ml) cream

1 tablespoon fresh lemon juice

Chopped chives, for garnish

Cut the leek tops off where they begin to thicken and turn green. Slit each leek down the middle from the cut end to just above the intact root end. Submerge the leeks in cold water and rinse the layers to remove any grit. Dry. Slice the leeks crosswise very thinly.

In a saucepan over medium heat, heat the olive oil. Add the sliced leeks. Cover and let the leeks sweat over gentle heat for 5 minutes. Uncover and cook 5 minutes more, until the leeks are softened. Add the potato slices and stock. Bring to a simmer. Cook until the potatoes are tender, about 10 minutes. Taste and add salt and pepper as needed. Cool the soup a little and blend in batches until very fine. Pass it through a strainer into a deep bowl. Add the cream to the cool, strained soup and stir very well. Add the lemon juice and taste again, adding a little more salt if needed. Chill thoroughly and stir well before serving.

Roast Asparagus

Served cold with mayonnaise, sliced thinly and tossed, raw, in a vinaigrette, pureed into a cold soup, folded into a cool mousse—local asparagus are at their peak. Serve hot or cool.

≪ SERVES FOUR ≫

1 bunch asparagus

2 tablespoons olive oil

2 tablespoons lemon juice

Salt and pepper

Preheat the oven to 450°F (220°C).

Snap off the bottoms of the asparagus if they are tough. Lay the asparagus spears in a single layer in a roasting pan or rimmed baking sheet and sprinkle the olive oil over them, followed by the lemon juice. Season well with salt and pepper. Add ¼ cup (60 ml) water to the pan. Roast, shaking the pan a couple of times, until just tender, about 15 minutes. Remove. Eat.

Strawberries with Prosecco

There are no quantities given—they are up to you. Only one caveat: The strawberries must be perfectly ripe.

Place a handful of strawberries in individual bowls. (I pick the fruit literally right before serving.) Sprinkle the berries with a little brown sugar. Pour over some cold prosecco. Each spoonful transforms in your mouth from whole berry to sweet juice mingling with the wine, epitomizing the ephemeral pleasure of seasonal eating.

The May farmers' markets are gorgeous. Ramps, rhubarb, asparagus, and strawberries arrive in succession. Long days and sunshine until after eight at night encourage an end to slow food and a return to simpler cooking and meals tuned to the rediscovered joy of eating outdoors.

The little stone table is scrubbed, a cloth laid across it, candles lit, and a jar of terrace flowers placed in front of the mirror that reflects all good things, including helpful candlelight. A chicken is marinating, waiting for the coals in the *braai* to acquire just the right hint of ash over glowing red. I pick a bunch of flat-leaf parsley.

Everything tastes better outside.

Gin and Bitter Lemon

Gin and Bitter Lemon season has begun, inspired originally by Gabriella Hamilton, who offered this combination at Prune, her restaurant on East 1st Street. Now I sip mine from nineteenth-century Woodstock—the first commercially made glass in South Africa, and in daily use (and peril) in our apartment—as I water the roof farm: check a plant, sip, pick some nasturtium leaves, sip. Touch the soil, sip.

« MAKES ONE DRINK »

**3 ounces
(6 tablespoons)
good gin**

Bitter lemon

Pour the gin over ice in a tall glass, and top with chilled bitter lemon. Add thin slices of lime and stir. This cannot be drunk indoors. Stick your head out of window to sip, if you must.

outdoor eating

Gin and Bitter Lemon

Nasturtium, Chive, and Avocado Salad

Four Alarm Roadkill Chicken with Avocado Cream

Strawberry Shortcake Fool

Nasturtium and Avocado Salad

Nasturtiums are a wonderfood, stuffed with anti-everything properties: antibiotic, antifungal, antiseptic. They are small green medicine chests and immunity boosters. My mother used to tell me to wrap some cheese inside a nasturtium leaf to help cure a sore throat, and I would walk round the garden solemnly, curing myself. It's a good snack, too. Piled on avocado, they are a bold foil for its green creaminess. Substitute any peppery leaf, such as young mustard or arugula, if you are not growing your own nasturtiums. (But grow your own nasturtiums.)

≪ SERVES TWO ≫

1 ripe Hass avocado, pitted, peeled, and cubed

1 cup (55 g) loosely packed nasturtium leaves

SHERRY VINAIGRETTE FOR A VERY SMALL SALAD

1 teaspoon sherry vinegar

Pinch of sugar

Salt

1 tablespoon extra-virgin olive oil

6 turns of a pepper mill

Just before serving, pile the avocado pieces in the middle of a bowl or serving plate. Heap the greens on top.

In a small bowl, whisk the vinaigrette ingredients. Drizzle over the salad.

Four-Alarm Roadkill Chicken with Avocado Cream

With a name like that it better be good. It is.

Whether cooked under a blazing hot broiler in a pan to catch the juices, or grilled over a fire, this disconcertingly flat chicken has become a versatile standard in our house. Traditional spatchcocking—cutting the bird down the backbone—still leaves the bloody (literally) question of how to cook the thigh and drumstick area through without scorching and drying the rest of the bird over one-directional heat. This method of splitting the entire breast from the body solves the problem. The wonderful bonus is crispy skin, all over.

Use a very sharp little knife (my high-carbon, $10 Opinel is perfect) or poultry shears to cut straight back through the rib cage from the cavity, moving all the way back to above the wing joint. Repeat on the other side. This separates the breasts and breastbone from the rest of the bony carcass—the thighs, legs, wings, and back. Now pull that breast section back and flatten the whole bird as if it were a new, thick book open to the middle page for the first time. You'll hear a little crack. You now have an extra long chicken, but one where the heat can reach in and cook every part evenly.

If you want to feed hungry friends—the best sort—you may need two chickens. In that case, double the marinade quantities.

≪ **SERVES TWO (WITH LEFTOVERS)** ≫

1 medium chicken, split as directed above	Juice of 3 limes (about ⅓ cup / 80 ml)	5 tablespoons (20 g) finely chopped parsley	Freshly ground black pepper
6 garlic cloves, finely chopped	1 tablespoon hot chile flakes, or 3 small fresh chiles, chopped	Salt	Avocado Cream, for serving (see page 98)

In a large flat dish or large bowl place your split-apart chicken. If it can lie flat, good—if it can't, not to worry. Toss the garlic, lime juice, chile, and parsley over the bird. Season generously with the salt and pepper. With your hands, turn the chicken over several times to distribute the ingredients and their flavors well. (Wash your hands afterward.) Place the chicken in the refrigerator to marinate, covered, for at least 1 hour and up to 12, if you are a good planner.

If you are using a broiler, transfer the chicken and its marinade to a shallow roasting pan. The chicken should be stretched out in the pan, skin side down. Preheat the broiler. When hot, cook the chicken for 20 to 25 minutes. When it is good and dark brown, and the pan juices are sizzling, turn it, just once. Baste the skin side with the juices. Cook for another 20 to 25 minutes, until the skin is dark brown and crispy, with a few charred spots. If the pan looks dry, add a little water—the sticky, tart juices are delectable. Remove the chicken from the oven and allow it to rest in the pan for 10 minutes. Carve the chicken into joints, slice each breast, and serve in a wide dish, with the pan juices spooned over the top.

If you are grilling over coals, use plenty of hardwood charcoal, and wait until a fine layer of ash has formed over red coals before transferring the chicken to the grill. Cook the chicken about 4 inches (10 cm) above the coals, starting with the inside down (it can take more abuse than the skin side, and the fire will be hotter at the beginning of cooking) and checking periodically that dripping fat does not ignite flames. After about 20 minutes, flip the chicken and cook for 20 to 25 minutes more, until the skin is dark brown and crispy, with a few charred spots. Transfer the *braaied* chicken to a large platter. Cut the bird into pieces, carve the breasts and slice them, rearrange them on a warm plate, and spoon any juices from the platter over the top.

Once you reach the deliciously crisp and sticky parts of the wing tips and back, which are mostly skin and morsels of tender meat, this becomes food for eating with your hands. The genteel might like a finger bowl. Provide large napkins and serve with the avocado cream alongside.

Avocado Cream

A creamy mouthful for the spicy chicken.

≪ MAKES ABOUT ½ CUP (120 ML) ≫

½ ripe Hass avocado, pitted, peeled, and cubed	2 tablespoons mayonnaise	Salt
	1 tablespoon fresh lemon juice	Freshly ground black pepper

In a small bowl, mash the avocado into a cream. With a fork, work in the mayonnaise and lemon juice. Taste and season with salt and pepper.

Strawberry Shortcake Fool

The perfume of local strawberries will remind you that the ubiquitous, rigid berries you see year-round in stores have no right to the name strawberry. My own plants provide handfuls of berries through the year, but I can't resist buying more, en masse.

Pâte sablée is a rich shortcrust pastry that I use again and again for desserts involving fruit, filled with wobbly custards or with whipped cream. It is heavy on butter, very light in texture, crisp and delicate. A little goes a long way. It pairs sublimely with very ripe, soft strawberries and is a decadent partner for fresh strawberry sauce.

For this cross between a tart, a trifle, and a fool I break up the baked, brittle pastry into shards and layer it with whipped cream and strawberries in coupes. For this dessert you need about a quarter of the pastry that this recipe yields. I freeze the remainder in individual, flattened balls for later use as shells for tarts that hold custard or flat discs onto which I heap fresh raspberries reclining on a pillow of whipped cream or Greek yogurt. Otherwise you could use it all at once, cutting out and baking many flat, delicious cookies.

《 **SERVES TWO** 》

FOR THE PÂTE SABLÉE

1 cup (200 g) unsalted butter

¾ cup (100 g) confectioners' sugar

2 egg yolks

1 drop vanilla extract

Salt (if using unsalted butter)

2 cups (250 g) flour

FOR THE STRAWBERRIES

1 cup strawberries

1 tablespoon sugar

Squeeze of fresh lemon juice

FOR THE CREAM

⅔ cup (160 ml) whipping cream

2 teaspoons superfine sugar

Make the *pâte sablée*: Grate the butter into a large bowl and allow to soften a little. Work the confectioners' sugar into the butter. Stir in the egg yolks and vanilla. Add the salt. Gradually add the flour until you have a ball of pastry. Be gentle and do not overwork it. Divide the ball in quarters, wrap each in parchment paper, and refrigerate, or freeze for later use. Refrigerate the piece you are using for 1 hour before rolling it out.

Preheat the oven to 400°F (200°C). Lightly butter a baking sheet.

On a lightly floured work surface, flatten the pastry a little with your hand. With a rolling pin, roll the pastry away from you, giving it a quarter turn every time. Repeat until it is about ⅟₁₆ inch (1.5 mm) thick.

Using a pastry cutter, press out several discs about 3 inches (7.5 cm) across. Lift each with a spatula onto the prepared baking sheet. Bake until the pastry is barely golden, about 8 minutes. Allow the discs to cool for a few minutes on the tray—until they are cool, they remain very flexible and fragile. Lift

them carefully off the tray onto a wire rack to finish cooling. The pastry can be baked up to 2 days in advance, then stored in a sealed container until needed.

Make the strawberries: Rinse and hull the berries, in that order. If you remove their green tops and then rinse them they will turn soggy. Dry them gently and well. Mash half the berries with the sugar and lemon juice. Transfer this rough sauce to a bowl. Of the remaining berries cut any large ones in half and put them with the rest of the berries into the sauce. Allow them to macerate for a couple of hours, chilled.

Make the cream: Whip the cream with the sugar until it forms soft peaks. Chill.

Just before serving, break 3 of the pastry cookies gently into large-ish pieces. In coupes or pretty glass bowls layer the cookies with the whipped cream and macerated strawberries. Serve at once.

Later, in raspberry season, use raspberries instead.

If you have baked a lot of cookies, using all the pastry, they can easily be a more formal dessert:

Top a cookie with a layer of whole, evenly sized fruit, and top with another cookie, which balances on the strawberries beneath to make a house. Dust with confectioner's sugar. Serve with a small fork and spoon, and extra sauce on the side. Perfect buttery crumbliness collapses into red pools of ripe fruit.

JUNE

This is the scarlet season.

In Brooklyn Bridge Park the slender branches of serviceberry trees hang low with ripe fruit early in the month. The little pomes—inverted coronets—taste sweet when red and applesauce-ish when purple. It is easy to browse quietly for a secluded hour here on urban fruit within arms' reach. At Pier 6 a bus driver waiting for the start of his shift beside his bus asks, as he sees me reaching up for more, Are those things *edible*? Yes, sir, I say, they are indeed. As I walk up the low hill at the western extremity of Atlantic Avenue and turn down shaded Henry Street toward home, I think about serviceberry pie, a highlight of my foraging year. I think the bus driver might like it. He might like serviceberry pancakes better, though. What is more American? Pie, period? Or pancakes for breakfast?

At Borough Hall in a light rain, behind the small park where lavender and Fairy roses spill wetly through the wrought-iron fence in a sea of green boxwood, the farmers' market's stream of strawberries is replaced by raspberries, glistening red currants, and cherries. Slender pink stalks of rhubarb tip from packing cases. The produce comes from farms up the Hudson Valley and across the river in New Jersey, picked in the last few days, packed in the dark mornings, and trucked in across bridges and through long tunnels to the city. I collect a bagful of red currants for jam and infused gin and a bouquet of succulent purslane for lunch.

On my way to collect milkweed near home, telltale sidewalk litter makes me look up. Mulberries! I have stumbled upon a pair of large trees and find myself diverted by the fruit whose purple stains on my hands and feet put me straight back under Mrs. Du Toit's next-door tree in Bloemfontein, where I was sent to fill a Pyrex bowl to carry home for dessert, to be served with cream. Or better, Mrs. Newton's tree on Waverley Road, with branches as sturdy as beams beneath my small bare feet, and whose fruit resembled giant, articulated purple caterpillars.

It will be a week of pies.

June brings the scent I have been waiting for. One evening, standing on the terrace, I know that the linden flowers have opened. Four floors up, the air is fruity and soft. The whole city, if it stopped for a second to inhale, would smell this right now. The little-leaf lindens open first, their creamy, furred clusters dropping scent onto the sidewalks. Enormous big-leaf lindens, or basswood, grow on the edge of Cobble Hill Park, half a block away. The bluestone beneath them lies in the deep shade created by their overlapping, heart-shaped leaves. They are a tree with a secret, shared only in June, when their small waxy flowers, hidden and intensely fragrant in suspended clusters beneath the silver-bottomed foliage, open.

On a hot day when the water of the harbor looks blue we embark on an epic walk from Piet Oudolf's gardens under the plane trees of the Battery Bosque at the southern tip of Manhattan, up, past the trimmed lawns where giant purple alliums lean towards the water, around, past the South Cove where countrified city pigeons feed on ripe fruit in the branches of the serviceberries growing beneath tall locust trees, along the leafy Esplanade with its rows of trees and shade gardens. We skirt the North Cove and its luxury yachts, walk through Teardrop Park, hidden between skyscraping eco-friendly apartment buildings and their green roofs, up along the baking West Side Highway, skirting riverside parks of waving grasses, and the flat wide, milky river, and veer east toward West 12th Street, where the striking Eremurus have begun to bloom in the Chelsea Meadows section of the High Line, the most populous and most glamorous of New York City parks, by far. We walk its length up to 30th Street, elevated above the western edge of Manhattan, before riding the air-conditioned subway all the way home.

The month heats up. The goldenrain tree in Cobble Hill Park is alight with yellow flowers that drop a week later to make bright, right-angled rivers in the spaces between the pavers on the sidewalk beneath. Orange daylilies are open and pushing their day-long trumpets through the black iron railings. In Red Hook the winter-dead garden at Pier 44 has disappeared beneath mounds of blue catnip and tall spikes of creamy yucca.

I walk home along Henry Street and its bike lane, now a long summer tunnel beneath meeting trees. The air is thick. Apricots are ripening on the tree in the playground a block away from home. My big canvas shopping bags are full. I have found black raspberries.

There are meals to plan.

Serviceberry Pie

We eat at least one warm serviceberry pie in June. Its distinctive almond undertone, released by the small seeds inside the red and purple berries, is the taste of early summer. As a foreign-born, naturalized American, I regard pie as edible Americana.

My mother and grandmother used this crust for apple pie. I use it now for every kind of pie. The pastry does not have to rest and is surprisingly delicate. The original recipe called for margarine. What can I say? Those were the wonder years. Mid-twentieth century. They believed.

≪ SERVES FOUR TO SIX ≫

FOR THE SERVICEBERRY FILLING

5 cups (500 g) serviceberries, stalks removed

½ cup (100 g) sugar

FOR THE PASTRY

¾ cup (175 g) unsalted butter

5 tablespoons (65 g) sugar

1 egg, lightly beaten

2 cups (250 g) flour

2 teaspoons baking powder

Pinch of salt

Vanilla ice cream, for serving

Preheat the oven to 350°F (180°C). Grease a 7½-inch (19-cm) round pan.

Make the filling: In a saucepan, heat the berries and the sugar slowly, covered, taking care not to let them scorch. Once the berries start to exude juice, cook them for another 5 minutes, shaking the pan every now then. Remove from the heat and set the filling aside to cool. Strain off the syrup and reserve it for another use (i.e., cocktails! See page 115).

Make the pastry: In a bowl, beat the butter and sugar until light and fluffy. Add the egg, along with a dusting of flour. Beat again. Gradually beat in the flour, baking powder, and salt. Once the dough comes together, divide it into two pieces, one twice the size of the other. The dough can be rolled out at once, or chilled until needed. Roll the larger piece of dough into a thin disc large enough to line the bottom and sides of the prepared pan. Press the dough gently into place. Roll out the second piece of pastry to cover the top of the pie. Fill the pie with the cooled berries and place the top crust over the filling. Crimp the edges by pushing the sides of the pastry top into the sides of the pastry lining the pan. Make several slits in the pastry top to allow steam to escape. Bake the pie until pale golden and crisp, about 30 minutes.

Serve with very good vanilla ice cream.

Beautiful June.

Abraham Darby continues its first flush, the large flowers bowed by the weight of their petals. Beside the rose the pink and apricot spires of Mexican hyssop attract a profusion of small flying pollinators. The basil begins to resemble the mature herb at last: purple and an interesting mottled green. I nip the growing tips repeatedly to encourage full, fat plants.

We eat more strawberries, and I feed the clever plants, hoping for sweet returns on a fishy investment. I use a bottle of diluted fish and seaweed fertilizer on the terrace every month. Then I have to shut the sliding door for a day, or hold my breath. When the next strawberry crop matures the berries are fatter and shining with ripeness.

The gloriosa lilies begin to open. The strange white tubers—like fat pencils—give rise to stems that are already five feet long, each leaf tip equipped with a cunning prehensile tendril that lassoes any support it senses. The buds are green, like sinister little masks, and they turn pale yellow before flaring open. Each day, their color intensifies until the lovely, recurved petals are an intense pink, before they relax, flattening and receding to a dull flat red.

The buds of the statuesque Silk Road lilies fatten and lengthen. One morning I find the first flower open. Its carmine throat is painted with lime, the long, highly suggestive pistil surrounded by five amber anthers which turn dusty and yellow as their pollen loosens. I tether the tall stems to prevent collapse—the lilies are heavy, like perfumed sails in a small breeze. Their pollen is a terrace hazard. After watering the garden I often discover, hours later, permanent acid-yellow stripes on my arms, or neck, or clothes. Nothing removes them. For days I live as one jaundiced.

At night the lilies' unstoppable perfume spills over the edge of the roof. Slow trails of nectar slide down their broad petals, luring moths who find this small garden among the roofs, sensitive to scent in the dark. The clear syrup is sweet and tastes like cloves.

The lilies announce summer, blooming in the best of it, even as the worst lies ahead. The longest day of the year has passed, and every day will begin to shorten even as the temperatures and oppressively damp heat increase. One day I pull the sliding door closed and turn on the air conditioner for the first time. The sound of the world outside disappears beneath its breathy hum. At night we turn on a fan to propel the cold air into our bedroom as we sleep. We are twice-cocooned from the sounds of the Brooklyn summer night. Ambulances, fire trucks, drunks, crickets, the morning robin chorus.

Several breba figs have ripened on the branches of the fig tree. They are huge, pendulous with their weight. I touch their increasingly smooth skins delicately each morning to test for ripeness. I pick the fattest at last, and eat it alone in the late afternoon, standing on the gravel of the terrace and pulling back the soft skin. It tastes like honey. Ten months of waiting are rewarded by the taste of that first fig, which summons and preserves a childhood where I climbed a tree higher than the roof of the house to eat the plump pink fruit, long ago and alone in the branches.

A cocozelle squash—a zucchini with racing stripes—turns almost overnight from a tiny vegetable to a huge bruiser, and we grill it in slices on the fire with squirts of lime juice. Beside it, small round calabacita squash swell, still attached to their flower petals. I have been picking handfuls of black raspberries and transparent white currants. The fava bean plants have made beans. This symbolic crop speaks eloquently of the true cycle of local seasons.

In the heat the shiso leaves, slow to start, are filling out at last but limp with heat. I pick them for wrapping around bites of barbecued short rib.

I pull the first potatoes. The pot yields a dozen new Yukon Golds.

The spring-planted garlic is ready. The new bulbs, with their cloves separated from each other by supple, delicate membranes, are smaller than their professionally grown counterparts but pink skinned and pungent.

We bring picnics up, lay a *kikoi* on the silvertop and set our places—forks, knives, pressed tin plates. The cat joins us. Sundown is now well after 8:00 P.M. We sit watching the glittering water, the small, slow ferries to Governor's Island. In the deepening sky above us the chimney swifts swoop. The air is warm well after dark.

I wake to a storm, lightning flickering in the gray morning light and thunder booming above. Hard drops of rain hit the skylights, percussive as hail. When the knitted and heavy sky begins to loosen and disperse, cumulus clumps pattern a perfect blue sky. Every plant on the terrace is defined and crisp, the colors bright. I can tell, standing on the inside of the double-paned glass of the sliding door, that there has been a change. I turn off the air conditioner and pull open the door. The air is cool.

We have been granted a reprieve.

Pigweed and Lamb's Quarter Tart

It may be a tart but it resembles a pizza. The difference is the dough, which is a miracle: flour and olive oil, and surprisingly flaky. Easiest thing ever.

I adapted this recipe from one of my most beloved—and most beautiful—cookbooks, Roger Vergé's *Entertaining in the French Style*. He makes a Swiss chard tart. I use the pigweed and lamb's quarters that I collect in Prospect Park or right outside, on the terrace.

≪ SERVES FOUR ≫

FOR THE PASTRY

2 ¼ cups (280 g) flour

Pinch of salt

½ cup (120 ml) extra-virgin olive oil

½ cup (120 ml) lukewarm water

FOR THE FILLING

¼ cup (60 ml) extra-virgin olive oil

2 shallots, thinly sliced

1 ½ pounds (680 g) lamb's quarter or pigweed leaves

1 tablespoon lemon juice

Salt and freshly ground black pepper

2 eggs

½ cup (120 ml) heavy cream

¾ cup (100 g) oil-cured black olives (pitted or not)

Make the pastry: In a large mixing bowl, combine the flour, salt, oil, and water and mix quickly. Form the dough into a ball, flatten it a little, wrap it in a very slightly damp cloth, and place in the refrigerator to chill for 30 minutes.

Make the filling: In a large sauté pan, heat the oil over medium heat. Add the shallots, letting them sweat for 5 to 8 minutes, until they take light color. Add the lamb's quarter or pigweed leaves and stir. Cover the pan for a minute to help the leaves steam, and then stir them again to wilt thoroughly. Add the lemon juice. Cook until the greens are just tender. Season with salt and pepper, and set aside to cool.

In a small bowl, whisk together the eggs, cream, and a pinch of salt.

Preheat the oven to 400°F (200°C). Grease a 16-inch (40-cm) baking sheet.

On a floured board, roll the pastry out into a large disc, wrap it around the rolling pin, and transfer it to the prepared baking sheet. Crimp up the edges to form a low border. Distribute the cooked leaves and shallots evenly across the surface of the dough. Scatter the olives over. Pour the egg and cream mixture evenly across the top, and slide the tray into the oven. Bake until the pastry is crisp, about 15 minutes. Eat hot or at room temperature.

Peach Wine Punch

For a meal as spicy as this one I allow myself to slum it with the wine: I consolidate the contents of two or three bottles that have been lurking in the fridge. A New Zealand sauvignon blanc, a Red Hook rosé, a viognier from Oregon.

Trust me.

I pour them into a carafe and add thinly sliced, very good peaches, as well as a tall stalk of mint. This is covered and chilled for a couple of hours, long enough for the peaches to give up some of their juice.

Mango and Avocado Salad

Fruit turns into something quite different when treated with fresh herbs, salt, and spice. This is healthy eating at its delicious best.

≪ SERVES TWO ≫

1 ripe Hass avocado, pitted, peeled, and cut into small chunks

Salt and freshly ground black pepper

½ large mango

Juice of ½ lime

Fresh cilantro, leaves only, washed and dried

1 fresh jalapeño, sliced into very thin rounds, with seeds

Pile the avocado into a serving bowl or plate. Season it with salt and pepper. Slice the mango thinly and top the avocado with the slices. Squeeze some of the lime juice over the fruit. Add the cilantro leaves and thin slices of jalapeño. Squeeze the rest of the lime over the salad and season again with salt and plenty of pepper.

Sweet and Spicy Shrimp

I love the strong flavors of Southeast Asia, with tart and hot and sweet all bouncing off one another in a single mouthful.

Head-on shrimp are best for grilling but they are very hard to find unless I go to Chinatown. The next best thing is to keep the tail shells on. If you can buy whole shrimp, all the better: The heads pack all the flavor.

Grilled shrimp cook quickly, needing only a small fire, or a flash in the pan if you have no fire. Perfect summer food.

≪ SERVES TWO ≫

24 medium shrimp, deveined but shells left on

½ cup (10 g) finely chopped cilantro stems

¼ cup (60 ml) fresh lime juice

3 tablespoons fish sauce

1 tablespoon finely chopped jalapeño

2 teaspoons sugar

2 tablespoons coconut oil (optional)

In a bowl, toss the cleaned shrimp with the cilantro, lime juice, fish sauce, jalapeño, and sugar. Cover and marinate in the fridge for a minimum of 1 hour or up to 3 hours.

Build a small fire in the grill. When the coals have formed a fine layer of gray ash, cook the shrimp for 4 or 5 minutes a side, until they are pink and opaque, periodically spooning the leftover marinade over the tails. (If you are cooking on a gas griddle or on the stove, heat the coconut oil until rippling and cook the shrimp, tossing, for about 5 minutes, until pink.)

Place the cooked shrimp into a bowl and eat at once, using your fingers.

JUNE MENU

Our meals are now almost always eaten outdoors—on the terrace at the stone table, on the roof, or at a nearby park, catching the breeze off the water. On warm days I avoid the kitchen and cook outside, the hot coals glowing beneath the coils of garlic scapes, asparagus, and the first summer squash from the roof, alongside a serious porterhouse, or the sizzle of a road-kill chicken.

Or these delectable short ribs. I like to wrap morsels of them in fragrant shiso leaves (known as sesame leaf in Korea).

Serviceberry Cocktail

The scarlet syrup that oozes from serviceberries destined for pie (see page 107) is the perfect excuse to mix an early summer evening cocktail with my go-to bubbly, prosecco. Strain the syrup from the pie berries and decant it into a small bottle. Keep refrigerated. It will last for months.

≪ MAKES ONE DRINK ≫

½ ounce (1 tablespoon)   Prosecco
serviceberry syrup

Measure the serviceberry syrup into a Champagne flute or coupe. Top with ice-cold prosecco.

cooking with fire

Serviceberry Cocktail

Green Bean and Parsley Salad

Beef Short Ribs and Garlic Scapes

Chocolate Roll

Green Bean and Parsley Salad

The first tender beans have begun to appear at markets. When I have blanched them, for this salad or for *salade niçoise*, I tend to gobble them greedily, straight from the strainer where they are draining, leaving too few for the designated salad. Fresh green or wax beans are delicately sweet and are easily a simple meal in themselves, heaped in a bowl and drizzled with good oil or a little pat of butter. How often do we feed ourselves that simply? Not often enough.

≪ SERVES SIX ≫

2 big handfuls of green beans, trimmed

FOR THE LEMON AND SESAME VINAIGRETTE

1 tablespoon fresh lemon juice

1 clove garlic, finely chopped

¼ teaspoon sugar

Salt and freshly ground black pepper

1 teaspoon sesame oil

2 tablespoons extra-virgin olive oil

1 tablespoon heavy cream

½ red onion, thinly sliced

1 bunch flat leaf parsley, leaves only

In a pot with a lid, boil water to which you have added 1 teaspoon of salt. Add the beans when the water begins to bubble. Blanch for 2 minutes, remove immediately and drain and refresh under cold water. Pat dry.

Make the vinaigrette: In a large bowl, whisk together the lemon juice, garlic, sugar, and salt and pepper to taste until the sugar is dissolved. Whisk in the oils until emulsified, then whisk in the cream.

Add the beans, onions, and parsley to the bowl and toss well. Season with additional pepper. Arrange in a serving bowl.

Beef Short Ribs and Garlic Scapes

It took me years to realize that short ribs could be grilled and remain succulent. They are one of my favorite things to eat.

FOR THE RIBS

6 big beef short ribs, on the bone

⅓ cup (80 ml) soy sauce

¼ cup (60 ml) fresh lime or lemon juice

1 tablespoon sugar

1 bunch scallions, finely chopped, green and white parts (about 1½ cups / 150 g)

1 thumb-size piece of ginger, peeled and sliced into matchsticks

FOR THE GARLIC SCAPES

1 bunch garlic scapes

2 tablespoons olive oil

1 tablespoon fresh lemon juice

Salt

Freshly ground black pepper

Make the ribs: Combine the ribs, soy sauce, lime or lemon juice, sugar, scallions, and ginger in a large bowl and allow the meat to marinate in the fridge for as long as you can, preferably 6 hours, turning the ribs a couple of times.

Make the scapes: Wash the scapes, dry them, and nip off the tough ends and any wilted heads. Toss them with the oil, lemon juice, and salt and pepper to taste.

Make a fire in the grill. When the coals have formed a fine layer of gray ash, place the ribs on the grill bone side down and grill for about 12 minutes. Watch for flames as the fat starts to drip, and move the ribs to the edges of the grill if there is a conflagration. Spoon the chunky bits of the marinade over the meat occasionally. Turn the ribs to cook the other side. Leave for another 10 to 12 minutes until the sides of the meat are no longer soft to the touch and the meat is dark brown.

While the ribs are cooking arrange the garlic scapes around them and turn frequently to prevent too much scorching. I never quite manage this. The scapes turn tender and sweet.

Remove the ribs to a plate and allow to rest for 10 minutes. Place the scapes on a serving platter.

Cut the meat from each bone and slice—do not lose the good juice. Plate and serve with the scapes and the delicious bones alongside, for primitive gnawing.

Chocolate Roll

This tender log stuffed with whipped cream looks clever and complicated. Clever it may be, but complicated it ain't.

<< SERVES SIX >>

FOR THE ROLL

5 eggs, separated

6 tablespoons (75 g) granulated sugar

5 tablespoons (27 g) cocoa powder

1 tablespoon flour

Pinch of salt

3 tablespoons milk

FOR THE FILLING

1 cup (240 ml) whipping cream

1 tablespoon superfine sugar

6 tablespoons (90 ml) red currant jam

Confectioners' sugar, for dusting

Preheat the oven to 350°F (180°C). Butter a rimmed baking sheet and line it with parchment paper, also lightly buttered. The paper must come up and just above the sides.

Make the roll: In a large bowl, whip the yolks with 4 tablespoons (50 g) of the granulated sugar until pale and thick. Stir in the cocoa powder, flour, salt, and milk. In another very clean bowl, whip the whites until softly fluffy and add the remaining 2 tablespoons granulated sugar. Continue whipping the whites until they form soft mounds.

Take a quarter of the whipped whites and cut them into the cocoa mixture with a spatula or large spoon. Add the rest of the whites, blending well but gently.

Pour the mixture into the prepared baking sheet, spreading it to touch all sides of the pan. Bake for 10 minutes and then check it. If the center is still very moist, give it another 2 minutes and check again. Remove from the oven and allow to cool in the baking sheet.

Loosen the edges of the parchment from the sheet with a butter knife. Cover the baking sheet with a damp dishcloth. Flip the baking sheet and cloth over in one smooth motion. Place the cloth and sheet on a work surface, cloth side down, and lift off the sheet. Peel the parchment paper from the cake.

Whip the cream with the sugar until stiff. Spread the cream evenly over the cake, and then dab the jam evenly over the cream.

Starting at one shorter side and using the lifted end of the dishcloth to push it along, start rolling the cake. Once the cake is in a log shape, transfer it very gently to a flat dish, seam side down, cover, and keep it cool until you need it.

Dust with confectioners' sugar at the last minute.

JULY

NEW YORK IN JULY

Average temperatures: 85°F / 68°F (29°C / 20°C)

The official average temperatures for New York in the month of July do not tell the real story. In fact, I'd be tempted to say, *they lie*. Sneak weeks of consecutive high 90s, with heat indices going berserk in New York's concrete and tar-topped jungle, turn the juggernaut of July into a clammy, clingy, real-life sauna whose only escape is either air conditioning or emigration.

And July comes around every year, despite our best intentions. Occasionally the latter stickiness of the month and the endless flat white sky are so bad that not even the lure of picnics in the long, daylit evenings can tempt us from our artificially chilled cocoon. We renege on dinner party invitations because no one can face the sweat of the subway and its platform temperatures that hover in the 100s.

Somehow, we survive. Plants have a lot to do with that.

In the city, July belongs to echinacea. The North American daisy is in ubiquitous and saturated bloom in parks and brownstone gardens where new cultivars flash carmine or orange, fluffed ruffles, double colors, or modest white petals drooping around exaggerated green cones. Bees and butterflies converge on the flowers that stand three feet tall and pink between streams of trucks and cars and yellow cabs.

All plants reach tropical proportions. Quirky edible gardens in the front yards of homes, in church grounds, and in community gardens are floral mirrors of the cultural background of their gardeners, transplants from Italy, Poland, the Caribbean, the Latin Americas, India, and the Midwest. In Kensington, one of the most culturally diverse neighborhoods in the city, yard-long purple hyacinth beans run up fences and green tomatoes stand guard in concrete driveways. The Greenest Block in Brooklyn Competition is under way, sponsored by the Brooklyn Botanic Garden, which sends clipboarded judges to score the relative horticultural merits of competing blocks. Across the enormous and sprawling borough, block associations vie for the title of the most floriferous. In a Caribbean neighborhood hot pink moss roses (portulaca) and purple petunias cascade from baskets wired high on street signs. Concrete urns on the sidewalk are filled with cannas and amaranth and the highly cultivated tree pits turn the sidewalk into a continuous garden. Rudbeckia and hydrangea and lilies squeeze through chain-link fences and march up stoop steps in dozens of pots. One block away there is nothing. The street is depressed, filled with unkempt front yards and bare chain link. It is another planet.

Along the summer beaches of the Far Rockaways new growth on the bayberries has turned them into green hedges flanking the wide, white beachside path under a glaring sun. I pocket the leaves to perfume a marinade. In the hot, brushy dunes early beach plums turn purple. I find yucca pods on the skeletal remains of their flower spikes and bring them home to pickle; other plants, more shaded, are still in bloom, their petals creamy and crisp as iceberg lettuce. Above the high-tide line native sea rocket is wasabi in leaf form—a herb whose pungent salad brings tears to the eyes. Milkweed has pointed and warty green pods, excellent pan-roasted with a pinch of cumin and sumac.

Farmers' markets have moved into high gear. Field-grown tomatoes arrive from New Jersey. For the first time, I have refrained all year from buying hothouse tomatoes from Canada. I choose the big fruit carefully. Will these really taste different? asks a worried man beside me. Yes, I say, they will. Privately, I hope it's true. The tomatoes are heavy and they cost a lot. But I can't wait. These will be supper, stuffed with fragrant rice and dill and small currants and pine nuts. It is a meal I will repeat for months, never tiring of it, happy to be gorging myself after such a long fast.

The market tables have become complex canvasses. Red fruits continue to arrive: cherries, shining red currants. There is a yellow and red heap of the first freestone peaches. My shopper's temptation is exacerbated by green gooseberries and succulent black currants, grown and sold by Wilklow Orchards. My mouth waters. My bags are full, but I have been waiting for this. Every year I buy black currants for mouthpuckeringly tart jam that is eked out through the year, and for infused gin, which turns a deep purple, redolent of the fruit—a homemade crème de cassis. I choose my little blue boxes of fruit, load up, and stagger toward home, stopping at Sahadi's to squeeze in the rice and pine nuts on the way.

In the cool, air-conditioned apartment I stand at the kitchen counter, free of my burden, and wolf the tart and musky berries compulsively, straight from their bag, stuffing my mouth with the intensity of summer at its bursting point.

Stuffed Tomatoes

I crave this dish. The recipe is based on one given to me by my friend Bevan Christie who lives, cooks, and eats in Istanbul. Bevan hates basmati and recommends baldo rice, which is hard to find in my neck of the woods. I don't think that basmati tastes like "wet burlap" as he does, but Bevan is usually right, so do try to source baldo if you can.

These tomatoes are equally good hot or at room temperature for a picnic or a cool supper, later in the week. Vegans, venture nearer.

≪ **SERVES TWO** ≫

4 large or 6 medium tomatoes

Salt

¼ cup (60 ml) olive oil

1 medium onion, finely chopped

¾ cup (140 g) basmati rice

2 tablespoons pine nuts (see Note)

½ teaspoon sugar

2 tablespoons currants

Freshly ground black pepper

5 whole allspice berries

¼ cup (10 g) chopped dill

2 tablespoons chopped mint

Preheat the oven to 400°F (200°C).

Cut the tomato tops to form a lid. Scoop out the flesh; chop it and reserve it in a bowl. Salt the insides of the tomatoes. In a sauté pan over medium heat, heat 2 tablespoons of the oil. Sauté half the onion until golden. Add the rice and the pine nuts and stir until glistening. Add the chopped tomato flesh and any juices in the bowl and ¾ cup (180 ml) of water along with a generous pinch of salt, the sugar, currants, a generous dose of pepper, and the allspice.

Bring the liquid to a boil, then cover and reduce the heat to low. Cook until the liquid is absorbed into the rice, about 15 minutes. Add the chopped dill and mint and mix well with a fork. Taste for salt and add a little more if necessary. Stuff the tomatoes. (There will be lots of leftover stuffing.) Place the tomatoes in a baking dish or pan and top them with their caps. Distribute the leftover rice mixture between the tomatoes in the dish and pour the remaining 2 tablespoons olive oil over everything.

Bake until the tops of the tomatoes begin to brown, about 40 minutes.

Note: Some people—myself included—experience an intensely bitter taste when eating pine nuts sourced in China. Consequently, I avoid Chinese pine nuts.

Picnics have turned blowsy and luxurious in the long evenings and are no longer the nipped and huddled lunchtime meetings of winter. Twenty minutes away on foot, the lawns of Pier 1 beckon.

Cucumber Soup

In the grips of a mega-heatwave with air quality alerts and heat advisories and air conditioners cranked to the max, and ironed-out cats and sweating husbands, I make cold cucumber soup and then we walk to find the breeze on the water. For picnics I transport it—chilled—in reusable hinge-top bottles or a flask.

❮❮ SERVES FOUR ❯❯

2 medium (10-inch- / 25-cm-long) cucumbers, peeled, seeded, and chopped (about 3 cups / 400 g)	1 teaspoon sugar
	2 cups (480 ml) vegetable stock
2 cloves garlic, ground into a paste with a pinch of salt	1 cup (240 ml) plain yogurt or buttermilk (omit the vinegar if using buttermilk)
3 scallions, white parts only, chopped	2 teaspoons white wine vinegar
10 fresh mint leaves	Salt
	Freshly ground black pepper

Blend the cucumbers, garlic, scallions, mint, sugar, stock, yogurt, and vinegar until smooth, working in batches. Taste for seasoning, adding salt and pepper as necessary.

Chill it thoroughly, covered, in the refrigerator.

Peas with Dill and Olive Oil

I first tasted these peas in Ayvalik, a pretty town on the Aegean, sitting with my friend Bevan Christie and his friend Lale under a bower of jasmine in her garden. It was idyllic, a rare moment. Lale set our small lunch table with linen and silver. We drank cold wine and cold beer, and she placed before us plates onto which she scooped heaps of green peas laced with whiskers of dill from a large glass jar.

Years later I thought about those peas and made them on a whim, cooking them for longer than you would think necessary. These are not the emerald of just-cooked peas. The longer cooking turns them khaki and sweetly complex and fragrant with the herbs and olive oil. I eat them on their own as a meal. Later I learned that Lale adds lots of young garlic or scallions to her peas at the start—try it, it's good. For this version, I keep it simple, and I use lemon juice, too. Because I can't help myself . . .

❮❮ SERVES FOUR ❯❯

3 cups (435 g) shelled peas	2 tablespoons fresh lemon juice
⅓ cup (80 ml) extra-virgin olive oil	1 bunch dill
	1 teaspoon sugar
	Salt

In a saucepan, combine the peas, olive oil, and lemon juice over high heat. Add enough water to cover the peas and bring to a simmer. Add the dill and sugar, cover, lower the heat, and keep the mixture at a simmer for 30 minutes. Add more water if necessary. At the end of the cooking time, raise the lid to allow any extra moisture to cook off. Add salt, stir well, and taste, adding more salt if necessary. Serve at room temperature.

Meatballs with Pine Nuts and Summer Savory

Nothing travels quite as well as a meatball. I adore them. Their variety is endless. Here I use the prolific and flavorful summer savory growing on the terrace and roof.

« SERVES FOUR »

½ cup (120 ml) milk

½ cup (55 g) bread crumbs

1½ pounds (680 g) ground lamb

⅓ cup (45 g) pine nuts (see page 125)

½ teaspoon salt

1 cup (100 g) chopped scallions, green parts only

2 cloves garlic, very finely chopped

2 tablespoons chopped fresh summer savory (or substitute fresh parsley or oregano)

2 tablespoons pomegranate molasses

1 egg

¼ cup (60 ml) olive oil

Pour the milk onto the bread crumbs and let them absorb the liquid for about 3 minutes. Squeeze them out and reserve.

In a large bowl, combine all the ingredients except the olive oil and mix very well. If you have time, leave the bowl in the fridge for an hour to allow the flavors to blend. Heat the oil in a heavy-bottomed pan. Start forming the lamb mixture into small balls the size of ping-pong balls. Fry until brown on one side, flip, brown, and remove to a plate when cooked. Cook in 3 or 4 batches and do not overcrowd the pan or it will lose heat and you'll get gray, steamed meatballs. *Shudder.*

Alternatively, preheat the oven to 450°F (230°C) and roast the meatballs on an oiled rimmed baking sheet for 15 minutes, turning once.

Serve the meatballs at room temperature.

Cherry Clafoutis

My mother made clafoutis often, usually with canned cherries. To us the word sounded like *platvoetjies*, meaning "little flat feet" in Afrikaans, so that is what we called it.

« SERVES FOUR »

2 cups (310 g) pitted ripe cherries (or enough to cover the bottom of the dish)

2 eggs

3 tablespoons sugar

2 tablespoons flour

Pinch of salt

1¼ cups (300 ml) whole milk (see Note)

2 drops vanilla extract

1 tablespoon kirsch (optional)

Preheat the oven to 350°F (180°C).

Lightly butter a round, shallow quiche dish. Scatter the cherries evenly across the bottom. Whisk together the eggs, sugar, flour, salt, and milk until smooth. Add the vanilla extract and kirsch, if using, and pour gently over the cherries.

Bake until just set, about 35 minutes (the middle should barely quiver when the dish is lightly shaken).

Note: For a more indulgent batter, substitute ¼ cup (60 ml) heavy cream for the same quantity of whole milk.

THE JULY
TERRACE

After irreproachable June, temperatures do not rise so much as expand and fill every available space. Humidity presses down and envelopes the terrace in a heat which flattens perspective and sucks the color out of the sky. Stepping outside is like entering an oven. The sliding door to the terrace remains closed. Our tiny apartment contracts again while summer hangs above us like a steaming death star.

These are long, long, hot days, with a steady watering of the pots, sometimes twice daily. The potent combination of daylight, heat, and water creates an explosion of growth. The herbs in July are at last luxuriant and every meal is dominated by one or the other, or all of them, chopped together. Our meals profit from them:

An oregano-spiked, butterflied leg of lamb, summer savory–rubbed baby back ribs, *salade niçoise* littered with basil and parsley, salsa verde singing with parsley and cilantro, and chilly vichyssoise fringed with snipped chives. Mushrooms à la Grecque swim with fennel and parsley and thyme and garlic. And there are pigweed crostini. The weed is delicious, given a flash in a pan with some olive oil, garlic, and lemon juice. Cold watermelon soup is heady with basil leaves, and basil tops buffalo mozzarella with the first of a succession of wonderful tomatoes from the roof.

The basil of July is purple and spotted, and my favorite. It forms a cool pool of contrast for the herbs and flowers around it and is smaller than the later-maturing Thai basil. Beyond it on the terrace edge the echinacea is a shock of pink. The sunlight is threaded with the flight of small insects whose patterns of approach and takeoff mirror in miniature the movement of massive aircraft on approach to or departure from LaGuardia, JFK, and Newark. Hornets, many species of bees, iridescent little flies, and butterflies work until dusk, not ceasing until they hand over to the moths, who arrive to sip nectar until the moon begins to set. By day, as I water and move the leaves of plants on the terrace, these sleeping moths start up from their hiding places, flying blindly into the light and fleeing to the canopies of the four oaks across the road. Above the terrace cumulus clouds march east.

It is another month of lilies. The petals of pale yellow Turks caps flare demurely beneath a raucous gaggle of Dunyazades whose louche appearance rewards close inspection. Lime, yellow, white, and hot pink are striped on the heavily beaded interior surface of each petal, designed, it seems, for those who read color in braille. Their pollen continues to give me electric, unwashable war stripes.

Eastern tiger swallowtail butterflies appear every summer, drawn to the parsley and fennel. Their plush, voracious offspring appall me. They eat my parsley. After the first year of war I learned to compromise by planting more. Eggs are laid, caterpillars follow, hatching from the single, tiny green dot deposited on the underside of a leaf. I check the leaves extremely carefully before washing them to eat.

During the day the silvertop of the roof farm burns my bare feet and I feel it even through the thin soles of the shoes I put on reluctantly. The edges of the black metal hatch to the roof are so hot in the middle of the day that I wear gloves to grip its edges if I have to do emergency daytime watering. The summer farm is best tended in the early evening.

Going to the roof when the sun's angle is low is like a small holiday now. It is not the terrace, all lush and contained. It is a little wild and primitive, urban in the company of satellite dishes and chimneys, and always fresher with a wind from the water. One's thoughts stray farther than usual, freed by the horizon and the view over New York Harbor.

The row of tomatoes, after months of slow growth, looks like a respectable hedge. Their green bulk makes the ragtag farm of early spring resemble a garden at last. By the end of the month I begin to harvest the Black Cherries, and a fat Black Krim, which is a revelation—dark green and red inside, intensely flavored.

Everything up here—the broad leaves of the summer squash, the flowering eggplants, the new green canes that will produce the black raspberries' second crop, the first ripe blueberries, the swelling fruits of the small watermelon—grows under a wide sky and an unimpeded sun. Herds of titanic clouds, each distinct and filled with storms, pass overhead. When they gather to drop warm rain, it fills the wide gutter that skirts the terrace to create a transparent moat in the sky. The rest of the water is absorbed by the thirsty plants, which continue to grow, and grow, and grow.

In the apricot-colored west a helicopter stutters toward its tour of the Statue of Liberty, passing above the brightly lit orange layer cake of the Staten Island ferry. Giant dragonflies appear in the twilight and zoom over the rooftops, smaller versions of the chimney swifts who are hunting closer to the water. After a picnic eaten late to avoid looking into the slipping sun, we stay on the roof in the dark and see a firefly light up once, twice, and then

the night is black again, stars above, and rows of moving lights on the water as ferries and taxis and tankers continue to carry people to where they want to go.

Fresh From the Roof

Blueberry Pancakes

Whether bought at market, collected from our own bush, or foraged from nearby Pier 6, I like blueberries best for breakfast. I separate yolks from whites and fluff up the whites to make a more buoyant pancake. This recipe works equally well with serviceberries in June. Or with slices of banana, for that matter.

SERVES TWO TO FOUR

1 cup (125 g) whole-wheat flour

1 cup (125 g) all-purpose flour

2 tablespoons sugar

1 tablespoon baking powder

¼ teaspoon salt

2 eggs, separated

1 ½ cups (360 ml) milk

1 cup (150 g) blueberries, rinsed and patted dry

Warmed maple syrup, for serving

Mix the flours, sugar, baking powder, and salt together in a large bowl. Whisk the egg whites until fluffy in a second bowl. Make a well in the dry ingredients and pour the egg yolks and the milk into it, and incorporate well. Add half the fluffed egg whites, folding them in. Add the second half of the egg whites and fold them in gently.

Drop a large spoonful of this batter onto a hot, well-buttered skillet. Once it has spread out to 3 to 4 inches (7.5 to 10 cm) across, scatter some blueberries over its surface. Flip each pancake when bubbles have risen and popped on the uncooked surface. Keep the cooked pancakes warm in a clean napkin while the rest are cooking. Serve in a stack with the maple syrup and good, strong coffee.

Dinner outside is a juggling act. Should we or shouldn't we? Will we die?

Much of our summer cooking is done outside, on the *braai*. I start the fire with paper, pack on hardwood charcoal, and then escape indoors as blue smoke billows. When I see an edge of gray dusting the molten coals, I venture out again, and commune with this primitive form of energy, which is also my favorite. We rarely entertain friends in the heat of summer, choosing to meet instead for picnics in a park. So this is a meal for two. My first crop of cured garlic almost always finds expression in this ritual combination of cold soup and warm ribs.

Cardinal

A Kir made with cold red wine becomes a Cardinal. It is surprisingly refreshing on a sultry night. My farmers' market black currants have been swimming in a bottle of good gin with sugar for two weeks and I unscrew the lid of the large mason jar for a premature taste (it is best after two months).

⟪ MAKES ONE DRINK ⟫

Light-bodied red wine, lightly chilled	1 ounce (1 tablespoon) crème de cassis	Slice of lime or sprig of basil, for garnish
Ice		

Pour the red wine into a tall glass over ice, and top with the crème de cassis. Add a slice of lime, or a sprig of crushed basil, and you have summer in your hand.

high summer supper

Cardinal

Ajo Blanco

Baby Back Ribs with Fresh Herb Rub

Squash and Bibb Lettuce Salad

Grilled Peaches with Mascarpone

Ajo Blanco

This Spanish soup, often called white gazpacho, is a restorative. Cool after hot, smooth after rough, simple after complicated. Ajo blanco contains no vegetables besides raw garlic, to which are added powdered (ground) almonds, some bread, chicken or vegetable stock, and the vital vinegar. It is one of my favorite things to eat (how often have I said that? I mean it every time), it is the key to my husband's heart, and I always make more than I need in a single sitting. Kept in the fridge in a jug it is a quick pick-me-up at any time of day or night, poured into a glass and sipped.

I use the garlic pulled in June from the roof.

≪ SERVES TWO ≫

4 slices white bread, crusts removed

½ cup (120 ml) milk

5 cloves garlic, peeled and crushed

5 cups (1.2 L) chicken or vegetable stock

2 tablespoons extra-virgin olive oil

½ pound (225 g) almond meal

1 tablespoon red wine vinegar plus extra (sherry vinegar is also good)

Salt

Freshly ground black pepper

1½ cups (140 g) grapes, cut in half and pips removed, for serving

Ice cubes, for serving

Soak the bread in the milk, then squeeze out the bread and discard the milk (*NO!* says the thirsty cat . . .). In a blender, put the garlic, 1 cup (240 ml) of the stock, the soaked bread, 1 tablespoon of the olive oil, and ¼ pound (115 g) of the almond meal. Blend well until smooth. Transfer to a large bowl and repeat with the remaining 4 cups (1 L) stock, 1 tablespoon oil, and ¼ pound (115 g) almond meal, adding it to the large bowl with the first batch once it is well blended. Whisk in the vinegar, and season with salt and pepper to taste. Cover the bowl and chill. Serve with a small handful of grapes and a couple ice cubes in each bowl.

Baby Back Ribs with Fresh Herb Rub

These neat little racks of ribs come from the top of the rib cage, above the spare ribs, and below the loin. Cooked like this they are good warm, the same night, or as gnawable leftovers the next day, if you can wait that long; they are excellent for messy picnics. I use two racks so that we have extra.

The herbs always vary according to the month and season, but this is my typical summer rub, when the summer savory is at its peak and when the terrace garlic is ready. If you cannot find savory (which is why I grow it), use rosemary and reduce the quantity to ¼ cup, as its oils are more pronounced.

While I usually cook these ribs over coals, they can also be put under a blazing broiler, if you can stand the heat in the kitchen, which in July I cannot. Either way, be sure to let them rest for at least 10 minutes afterward, leaving them tender and juicy before slicing.

≪ SERVES TWO ≫

⅓ cup (20 g) chopped summer savory (or substitute rosemary or thyme)

1 cup (60 g) chopped parsley (about 2 small bunches)

½ lemon or lime, very thinly sliced and then chopped (including the zest and pith)

Juice of 3 lemons

8 cloves garlic, finely chopped

3 tablespoons mustard

2 teaspoons brown sugar

2 racks baby back ribs

¼ teaspoon salt

Freshly ground black pepper

Combine the herbs, lemon or lime, lemon juice, garlic, mustard, and sugar in a bowl or mash them together on the chopping board to mix well.

Lay the ribs in a large, flat dish. Add the herb rub and massage it into the meat, covering both sides. Season heavily with black pepper and lightly with the salt. Leave to rest in the fridge for at least an hour, but remove the ribs half an hour before you are ready to start grilling.

Make a fire in the grill. When the coals have formed a fine layer of gray ash, add the ribs and cook them for about 12 minutes per side. Typically, by the time they are brown and are smelling mouth-wateringly good, they are ready.

Remove the ribs to a warm dish, tent with foil to allow some steam to escape, and let them rest for 10 minutes or longer. Slice each rib from the next and serve them from a communal bowl, piled high.

Squash and Bibb Lettuce Salad

Summer squash enjoy a six-week season on the roof. Young and raw, they have a delicate flavor and soft crunch that pairs well with fresh mozzarella and tender lettuce. My first cherry tomatoes make an appearance. And male squash flowers are good for two things: pollinating the females and then for the plate.

≪ SERVES TWO ≫

2 handfuls washed and dried Bibb or Boston lettuce

6 cherry tomatoes, halved or quartered

2 tender round squash, sliced paper thin, top to bottom

4 squash flowers, halved, lengthwise

½ ball (about 4 ½ ounces) fresh buffalo mozzarella

FOR THE WHITE WINE VINAIGRETTE WITH BASIL

2 teaspoons white wine vinegar

Pinch of sugar

Pinch of salt

Freshly ground black pepper

2 tablespoons extra-virgin olive oil

Basil leaves, torn up

Arrange the lettuce, tomatoes, squash, and squash flowers on a serving plate. Pull pieces of cheese from the soft mozzarella ball and distribute them among the leaves.

Make the vinaigrette: In a small bowl, whisk together the vinegar, sugar, salt, and pepper to taste until the sugar is dissolved. Whisk in the oil until emulsified, then stir in the basil.

Just before serving, drizzle the vinaigrette over the salad.

Grilled Peaches with Mascarpone

The first red-blushed yellow peaches are at market. They have nothing in common with the woody balls in supermarkets, which have often been chilled to indignity and whose skins develop a suspicious wrinkle on Day Two.

After sating myself (and the cat, who adores them) on the fresh peaches, with juice dripping, I turn the rest into a simple dessert by grilling them on the cooling fire. This amplifies their peachiness, which is offset by the incomparable richness of a dollop of mascarpone.

When I am fireless I prepare them in a ridged cast iron pan, which also gives them impressive stripes.

≪ SERVES TWO ≫

2 large yellow freestone peaches, unpeeled, split apart, pit removed

1 teaspoon sugar

2 tablespoons mascarpone

3 amaretti cookies, crumbled

Sprinkle the sugar over the cut side of the peaches and allow to sit for 5 minutes. In a hot griddle pan or over a cooling grill fire, cook the peaches face-down for 6 to 8 minutes, then turn them carefully to cook the skin side. The cut side will have caramelized beautifully. Cook another 6 to 8 minutes and transfer to a plate. Fill each hollow with mascarpone, and strew the crumbled amaretti cookies over the top.

AUGUST

NEW YORK IN AUGUST

The best thing about August is that the next month is September. August is why summer holidays and the Hamptons were invented. We don't take summer holidays. And we have no beach house. We have the terrace, the roof, and the city.

In early August the humidity of summer melts the city's populous collection of islands and rivers and waterways into a fractious and heat-damp mass. High above the grid, mountains of clouds pass on their way to the ocean, dwarfing the skyline and leaving it behind. When they pause above us, the rain they let loose is thick and fast and pins the streets in place. The sky joins with the rushing gutters and running streets. Afterward, for an hour or more, the air lifts, and is breathable.

We decided to reconnoiter Green-Wood Cemetery in August, thirsty for green on a hazy Sunday. Green-Wood's hills, rare in Brooklyn, can be seen from our roof, to the southeast. Beneath its trees, old and heavily leafed, shade is a dark, constant presence before autumn touches the oaks, beeches, and maples gorgeously. The R train takes us underground to 4th Avenue in Sunset Park, and a two block walk uphill puts us at Green-Wood's ornate gates guarding a mounded expanse of clipped lawn.

The crests of the green hills reveal unencumbered views of more green hills stippled with old stone headstones in a space that seems otherworldly and endless. The trees are revealed to be some of the most beautiful in the city. We stop and sit in the private shade of an old catalpa, its leaves like limp cloth, its branches arched toward the grass, and eat our sandwich picnic. Green monk parrots flit, screeching in faraway treetops, brief highlights against the varied and textured greens. The flowering panicles of tree hydrangeas are a foxed white beside the pale angels and weathered stones. We sit quietly, refugees seeking green. As we finish our lunch Vincent points to a low brown shape moving confidently through the short grass. It is a large and sleek groundhog, grazing contentedly and pausing often to sniff and inspect, undisturbed and unworried in his country.

All afternoon a storm has been gathering in the west over Jersey and an hour later it is above us, the air motionless, the light of its arrival sending the trees deep into relief, bringing the blurred edges of the summer day into sudden contrast. We turn back early as a violent downdraft shakes the branches around us, the storm bursting, the warm water emptying from the sky like arrows. We arrive at the subway with our clothes flapping wetly against our legs, cameras wrapped in anything we can spare. On the train dry passengers reassess the weather after glancing at us as briefly and impassively as only New Yorkers can. Hm, you can see them thinking, Rain.

In the interests of foraging, mid-month, we head out to Dead Horse Bay to find the beach plums whose blossoms filled me with anticipation in the spring. As we wait for the train at Borough Hall, sweat collects in the small of my back. The subway car is a refrigerated heaven. Surfacing on Flatbush Avenue, the heat is a new shock. Within minutes we are on a bus, cool as cucumbers again. It is filled with a New York cross section of beachgoers. Black, beige, brown, tattooed, skinny, fat, cool, indifferent, all armed with bags of towels and coolers of drinks. The bus drops the two of us in the middle of nowhere and carries its crowd to the Far Rockaways, leaving us to tramp into the anonymous bushes.

The first thing I see is ripe wild black cherries. Dark and glistening, strung like pearls on each side of a central stalk, they are unexpected and everywhere. I have never seen so many. They are sweet and bitter and wonderful for jam. If there are no beach plums, these are the compensation. Beside the wide paths the wild lettuce of spring is now five feet tall and in bloom, the thick leaves inedibly bitter. I find the field where I saw the plums and bushwhack my way through waist high milkweed and high summer growth. It is a new country, barely recognizable, and the beach plums have been obliterated by a tangle of invasive vines. The fruit I can see is tiny and pockmarked. I retrace my steps to the waiting Frenchman who is deeply suspicious of lurking poison ivy. Back at the cherries I strip handfuls into my brown paper packets and collect several pounds' worth. We walk down to the beach and I pick some heads of fresh, sticky staghorn sumac, to submerge in vodka and drink in December. On the cooler and windy beach, littered with broken glass from the last century and plastic from ours, the prolific sea rocket has set seed and I collect some of these too, to turn into pickles. The water of Jamaica Bay is the color of mud and the sky above it white without relief. A windsurfer whips over the dull chop on his board.

Back in the concrete bowels of Brooklyn, cultivated plums are streaming into farmers' markets and collecting in purple, red, and yellow mounds. At the height of the growing season the tables are buried beneath fruit and vegetables. I buy too much, unable to resist the glossy purple curves of eggplant,

one each of a dozen varieties of heirloom tomatoes, boxes of fat blueberries. Cosmos and zinnias and sunflowers packed into buckets are carried aloft by shoppers like prizes. Bruisable white peaches have arrived. I collect them very carefully. The air above their table hums with the scent of their juice. Signs exhort shoppers to eat entire yellow peaches before deciding whether to buy. Produce needs to be sold. Gluts demand consumption. I turn into an instant and reverent vegetarian and buy more ears of corn than we can eat in a sitting.

At home, I stand over the sink, slurping my first white peach, its sweetness flooding me with my childhood.

Forager's Special

Sumac in Vodka

A beautiful, peppery-sour mix for cocktails.

For a virgin version, cover the sumac with plain water and strain it through muslin the next day. Sweeten to taste and drink as you would lemonade. This can also be reduced (without sugar) to use in cooking as you might tamarind syrup or lemon juice. Store in the fridge.

≪ SERVES TWO ≫

2 heads fresh staghorn sumac	⅓ cup (65 g) sugar	1 bottle good vodka (I use Stolichnaya)

Break the sumac into florets and cut off as much of the green stems as you can reach. Do not rinse the sumac or you will lose the sour coating that is its charm.

Place the sticky sumac in a large jar, add the sugar, and pour the vodka in to cover. Seal. Swirl and tilt the jar to dissolve the sugar. The intensely sour sumac will flavor the vodka within days, but I strain mine off after 2 weeks, pouring the alcohol through 2 layers of muslin to strain out any fine hairs from the sumac. Store in a decanter where you can enjoy the gorgeous glowing amber color of the alcohol.

THE AUGUST TERRACE

Month of drama in the sky. August is moody. Days and nights when the air outside is like hot, sodden cotton wool alternate with brief transparencies of blue sky that offer a subliminal taste of autumn on their edges. Hurricane season is in the offing, and even New York is brushed by storms' outer bands as weakening systems whirl up the coast at full throttle.

The herbs on the edge of the terrace have become an uninterrupted mass of scented texture, interlocked and meshed into a lush, buzzing forest. Moss roses open early and fold by midday, their shock of color bright against the strawberries whose long stems leave the red fruit hanging over the edge of their pots. Above them, clouds billow like whipped cream.

The lemon basil, more delicate and heat sensitive than the rest, blooms first as I give up nipping out its buds. I keep its flower-studded spires for the bees, which bend the stems with their constant attention. The Thai basil on tall purple stems reaches its peak. Butterflies alight on the calamintha flowers and festoon the long-blooming agastache. I count more species than I have seen at one time: skippers, cabbage whites, painted ladies, monarchs, and moths. Bees and bright flies, unidentified and zooming, touch my hands lightly as my fingers interfere with their work, picking leaves for our supper while they collect their own.

On the parsley and the fennel the results of the eastern tiger swallow-tail's July egg laying appear. Caterpillars have emerged, striped and voracious. Despite their velvet beauty, I remain unamused, relocating some to one parsley plant they may decimate, and giving the rest flying lessons. Whee!

The main crop of figs is ripe at last, exactly when the purple clematis reblooms after its summer haircut. I collect a bowlful, trying to admire the fruit respectfully for a few hours before wolfing the lot in one sitting. I restrain myself and save most of them for a simple supper of paper-thin prosciutto and the halved fruit. In the following days I pick the remainder and we eat them with our tomatoes, a strange and good combination with mint and basil from the terrace. And then it is over. No more figs for a year. Just like that.

Heeding wind or hurricane warnings, we remove all the pots from the terrace edge in case some flying object dislodges one and sends it past the catchnet of the wide gutter to the courtyard below. The effort is backbreaking—lifting the pots and placing them on the terrace floor, and then doing it all in reverse when the threat has passed; but worse are the summer slugs that appear. When unfamiliar pots invade their leafy domain the hitherto hidden slugs discover new grazing grounds (strawberries! basil!). Beer traps are prepared. I am surprised by the number of bodies I collect, and a little sorry. But not very.

It rains. It starts loud and drums on the skylights, somewhere after midnight. I think of water washing horizontally some feet above us, heading for the gutters, pooling in the low corner. As the storms sit overhead, I am up on the roof in the wee hours as something metallic rolls around, loose. In the tugging, warm wind and water I find nothing and disappear down the hatch again, closing it behind me.

It rains while I stand on the terrace wrapped in a sodden *kikoi*, emptying water from the *braai*'s huge copper bowl, before flipping it upside down, to collect no more. It rains while we have breakfast. It rains all day.

And then it stops. Now, dry air, tugging wind, a collapsed New Dawn rose. I spend an afternoon on the roof, searching for weak spots, patching a suspect area with black cement, checking the gutter, and then moving on to more interesting things, like deadheading the shattered roses. As the day grows, the humidity returns, smothering us gradually with that old August feeling.

Escaping to the roof farm, I find long purple and fat white eggplants hanging below furred, spiked leaves. Black peppers are bursting from plants grown from seed. The first ground cherries are sweet inside their papery husks and rustle as I pluck them. Blueberries are ripe.

The little Yellow Pear tomatoes are so prolific that they threaten to topple their pot, which I wedge more securely. I find the first red Brandywine and gloat over my beautiful Green Zebras. The tomatoes' leaves are turning blighty but I am used to this. The fruit will still ripen. The Cherokee Purple and Black Krim fatten with juice and I eat them one evening when I am home alone. Two slices of brown bread slathered with mayonnaise, salt and pepper, the thick slices of tomato. August has its upside, and it lives in the juice of these, the best tasting tomatoes I have known. I will never forget this sandwich, nor the one I made the next night, with applewood-smoked bacon. I thought I knew how to eat, but it took this tiny farm on a rented roof in a big, big city to teach me the very basics:

First, catch your tomato.

Late in the month we eat our picnic supper on the roof—our tomatoes and our figs and our own grilled peppers with anchovies, with fresh bread. An electric chorus of cicadas rises to shimmering fever pitch in the trees in the back gardens ahead of us and the oaks behind, on the street, before receding in an exhausted wave, ending in a single, despondent click. We stay late, sipping wine and watching the sky firing its sunset changes in vivid parallel bands of high cloud in the west.

The light disorients me. It does not belong to summer. Times have changed, despite our vigilance. The season is slipping. Our eyes wander with the lights of a long barge heading slowly toward the East River, and we remain lost in thought, thinking of other waterways and other lights, and other possible lives waiting to be lived.

Fresh From the Roof

A Jugful of Gazpacho

This quintessential summer soup varies every time I make it, depending on what is on hand and what grows up top.

❰❰ SERVES TWO, OR FOUR AS AN APPETIZER ❱❱

4 medium ripe tomatoes	½ red pepper	8 basil leaves
1 medium cucumber, peeled and seeded	2 teaspoons sherry or red wine vinegar	½ cup (20 g) torn bread pieces (optional)
2 cloves garlic, peeled	1 teaspoon sugar	2 tablespoons olive oil (optional)
½ red onion	Salt and freshly ground black pepper	

Bring a pot of water to a boil. Slit the tops of the tomatoes with a sharp knife and place them in the boiling water for 1 minute. Drain and peel the tomatoes. Remove their woody stem base. Chop the cucumber, garlic, onion, and pepper roughly and place them in a blender. Add the remaining ingredients and blend until smooth. Taste for seasoning and add more salt and pepper if necessary. The flavor should be pungent but well balanced. Chill very well. Serve with a couple of ice cubes in each bowl.

The air conditioner does its expensive job while the terrace shimmers and the roof buckles and pops in the heat. If the air lifts, we head outside and dine again at the stone table. On the bad days we lurk indoors and eat large salads or food that I tend on the fire, separated from it by the insulation of that double-paned glass door.

Blackout Cocktail

In August of 2003, New York City experienced a spectacular blackout. Stuck in Manhattan on a subway whose first car had just crawled into the station, I emerged to find nothing working. No way home, except to walk across the Brooklyn Bridge with thousands of fellow New Yorkers, as cars stood bumper to bumper below us. The day was eerily reminiscent of 9/11 and I was nervous. It was a long, hot walk. I was wearing fancy shoes for a job interview. My feet were blistered when I got home. I went to the freezer and found the ice trays still intact, picked some mint from the window box, and mixed two strong drinks. I carried them downstairs to my neighbor, Constanza Jaramillo, whom I barely knew. We sat at her kitchen table with these drinks in the gathering dusk, and talked, and waited, and became friends.

≪ MAKES ONE DRINK ≫

Mint

2 teaspoons confectioners' sugar

2 ½ ounces (5 tablespoons) Cognac

½ ounce (1 tablespoon) fresh lemon juice

Sparkling water

Muddle the mint with the sugar in a tall glass. Add the Cognac and lemon juice. Stir. Top with sparkling water and lots of ice. Get to know thy neighbor.

late summer supper

Blackout Cocktail

Tomato and Fig Salad

Butterflied Leg of Lamb with Sour Cream and Garlic

Piyaz

Apricot Cake

Tomato and Fig Salad

I stumbled upon this combination by accident. I had tomatoes from the roof: Yellow Pear, Black Cherry, Mexican Heirloom, Green Zebra, Black Krim. I had figs (nameless) from the tree. Why not . . . ? Mint and basil pulled the two together, and we have never looked back.

My rooftop tomatoes have changed the way I shop and cook. Why? Because they changed the way I think. Day in, day out, winter or summer or fall, there are the generic round red tomatoes in grocery stores and supermarkets. I am not fundamentalist about it, but for the most part I am happy to wait for the real deal, to tune my cooking toward what is ripe, and to sate myself once my own small garden and the farmers' markets start to produce.

‹‹ SERVES SIX ››

1 cup (150 g) mixed heirloom cherry tomatoes, cut in half

2 cups (360 g) mixed larger tomatoes, quartered

6 figs, peeled and halved

Salt (not much)

Freshly ground black pepper

2 teaspoons fresh lemon juice

2 tablespoons extra-virgin olive oil

8 mint leaves, torn or sliced into ribbons

4 sprigs basil, leaves torn at the last minute

Arrange the tomatoes and figs in shallow bowl. Sprinkle salt and pepper over them. Whisk the lemon juice and olive oil and drizzle it over the salad just before serving. Top with the mint and basil leaves.

Butterflied Leg of Lamb with Sour Cream and Garlic

I have learned to ask for half a leg of lamb, and Pedro Franco, my butcher at Los Paisanos, obliges. If you are forced to buy a whole leg (a considerable investment), use half or even a third, depending on its size, for this butterflied recipe. Keep the rest for a curry or a roast. I take home the cut-up bones, too, and I use these as the base for a stock over which I cook stuffed Greek-style grape leaves. Or you can roast the bones and eat the marrow with a squeeze of lemon juice. But not everyone likes that as much as I do.

Marjoram has a higher, headier note than oregano, but both are surprisingly powerful. By August my marjoram is in bloom and I annoy the bees by using the flowers for this marinade. Rosemary is an obvious match for lamb, and I often use it instead.

« SERVES SIX »

½ leg of lamb (about 3 pounds / 1.3 kg), butterflied	2 cups (480 ml) sour cream 6 cloves garlic, finely chopped	3 tablespoons chopped marjoram or oregano (or 4 sprigs rosemary, needles only)	½ teaspoon salt Freshly ground black pepper

Place the butterflied lamb in a large bowl. Add the sour cream, garlic, herbs, salt, and pepper to taste. Massage the marinade into the lamb with your hands. It will feel funny but it is worth it. The longer you leave it to marinate, the better. I have managed 24 hours, but sometimes only 1 hour. Try for 12.

In good weather, I cook this over a fire. Otherwise, the broiler works very well, though I try hard to avoid it in August. Either way, each side of the meat needs to be exposed to even and high heat for 20 to 25 minutes for pink lamb. This means you need a pretty good fire to begin with, so that it can last. Once the lamb is very brown on both sides, remove it to a platter, cover, and allow the meat to rest for 10 to 15 minutes. The resulting juice is half the pleasure. Sometimes, while the lamb is resting, I toast some good bread over the embers and rub it with a clove of garlic, to sop up that juice. A habit is a habit.

After it has rested, slice the lamb into medium pieces and arrange them on the platter again, drizzling the juice over the top. You will lick your fingers.

Piyaz

Sunday night was kebab night at Anatoli, the beautiful Turkish restaurant, run by my friends Bevan Christie and Mustafa Candan, in Cape Town. Gone were the varying slow stews and melting chops and stuffed vegetables of the week before. Skewers would appear in the glass case to which customers would be guided to choose their main courses, spearing chunks of swordfish with bay leaves, chicken with sumac and chile, spicy ground beef. More importantly, there would be *piyaz*—a white bean salad spiked with onion, whose vinegary tahini sauce would soak into the delicious, buttery rice that accompanied the kebabs. It is something—and somewhere—I still crave.

❮❮ SERVES SIX ❯❯

3 tablespoons tahini

3 tablespoons sherry vinegar

Salt

Freshly ground black pepper

2 cans extra-large white beans, drained

1 small red onion, sliced fairly thin

Powdered sumac, for serving (optional)

Spoon the tahini into a small bowl. Add 3 tablespoons of water, little by little. Stir patiently until blended and smooth. Add the vinegar and stir until the dressing is pourable, but not watery. Add salt and pepper to taste. The salt brings out the best in the onion and counters the worst in the vinegar. The beans really suck it up, so don't be shy. Pour this dressing over the beans in a bowl. Add the onions and toss with your hands. If you do it with a spoon, you'll break the beans. Taste. More salt? More vinegar? Yes? Add. Put the salad in the fridge to chill. Sprinkle sumac over the top before eating, if you have it.

Apricot Cake

Local apricots arrive and depart faster than you can say "schnapps."

I love fruit in desserts. Calling this a cake is a little optimistic, as it is very rustic—meaning it looks like something went wrong—and more horizontal than vertical. But warm from the oven, the fruit heated to intensity, its flavor is hard to beat.

《 SERVES SIX 》

7 tablespoons (100 g) unsalted butter

½ cup (100 g) white sugar

2 eggs

6 tablespoons (45 g) flour

1 teaspoon baking powder

1 tablespoon apricot brandy or schnapps (see Note)

5 fresh apricots, halved, or sliced thickly

Preheat the oven to 350°F (180°C). Butter a 7½-inch (19-cm) round spring-form pan.

In a mixing bowl, cream the butter and sugar until pale. Add 1 egg and a dusting of flour and mix again. Add the second egg and more flour, and when that is smooth, add the rest of the flour and the baking powder, stirring very well until the mixture is smooth. Finally, blend in the brandy or schnapps.

Spread the apricots, cut side down, on the bottom of the prepared pan. I like concentric circles, but chaos is fine, too. Pour the cake batter over them and smooth it—it will just cover the apricots. Bake for 25 to 30 minutes, until lightly browned at the edges and firm to the touch. Remove from the oven, release the ring of the pan, and allow to cool. Transfer the cake to a serving plate. This is best eaten within a few hours. Good for breakfast the next day too, but avoid refrigerating it as it turns rather solid.

Note: To make your own apricot schnapps, cover sliced apricots (and 3 or 4 apricot kernels from inside the pit) with good vodka or eau de vie *in a big jar and leave them to become acquainted for a month. Strain through muslin and bottle the alcohol. The alcohol-infused fruit is delicious with whipped cream. What isn't?*

NEW YORK IN SEPTEMBER

Average temperatures: 77°F / 60°F (25°C / 16°C)

A clarity of light and air arrives. One morning, in the acute perspective that September gives to every building, roof, and tree, we know that summer is over. It is a relief.

The sky is an unrivalled blue. Every skyline is sharpened and defined. Streets are long and deep shadows are explicit. Colors are vibrant. Each exquisite silver scallop of the Chrysler Building is visible for miles as the dry, dense air that precedes cold weather penetrates the city and brings it into focus.

Summer's heat has brought a premature carpet of dry leaves to the bluestone sidewalks so that we crush them underfoot and smell a memory half extinct, barely accessible and long ago. We are scenting fall.

For the first time since June we walk outside without breaking into a sweat. At night the air has an edge that makes us think about what sweaters are for, and we discover moth holes in our favorite pullovers. Coats remain a distant memory, and hang like a threat in the closet.

At the farmers' markets a never-ending glut of tomatoes and late summer eggplants and corn still piles high on tables and is picked over fretfully by the same shoppers who pined for them all the long winter. Fickle, we are impatient for change. Early Seckel pears fill wooden crates. Round mountains of plums give me ideas. Concord grapes are ripe at last, in dark purple and green bloom. Honeybees hover over the musky syrup that oozes from spoiled and sampled bunches. I start to eat my grapes before I have reached the subway platform, the loose skins slipping onto my tongue and swallowed after the soft pulp. Walking in the labyrinth of tiled tunnels under Union Square, ducking lower into the retained heat that recalls soaking summer, this single mouthful puts me immediately beneath the Van Heerdens' grape arbor behind their house on Marquard Crescent in Bloemfontein, where as a little girl I first tasted the musk of Catawbas, a close Concord relative, and unusual in South Africa.

On a blue weekend we ride the A train, skimming the surface of Jamaica Bay where the tracks cross it on their way to the Far Rockaways. We disembark on the island of Broad Channel. It is a community of modest beach houses, low chain-link fences, clean streets, cemented front yards, BEWARE OF DOG signs guarding chipped garden gnomes who preside over gardens of gravel and fake flowers. Every wooden utility pole flies an American flag. You can hear a pin drop. On the wide Cross Bay Boulevard we take a right, and hike for another ten minutes down one of the worst-maintained and weed-sprouting sidewalks in the city and on to the Jamaica Bay Wildlife Refuge, whose two parts straddle the boulevard.

We turn sharply east, past the sign warning of deer ticks, into the shade through a tunnel of white birch trees. The city disappears. At Big John's Pond, a family of black-crowned night-herons dozes on a fallen branch tilting toward the water. A giant egret is frozen in fishing position above the lily pads.

On the East Pond, scores of white swans float in front of a palisade of trees beginning to tint orange and studded with roosting egrets. The ascending thunder of the jets across the water at JFK starts to feel like part of the weather. On a Sunday afternoon there is no one else in sight.

Here is goldenrod, the harbinger of fall, tilting above the last transparent flowers of purple false foxgloves. Nearby in the rain-fed grass are the low stems of nodding ladies' tresses, a clear white orchid. This is New York City.

The Refuge on the other side of the boulevard is another country—the wide open west. The air is a constant salted breeze off the bay. Small waves lap the beach where smooth cordgrass is a supple ruffle on the shoreline. At low tide the beach broadens and a walk around its damp skirt reveals clam shells, horseshoe crab skeletons as fortified as medieval body armor, emerald pieces of sea lettuce, and the ugly flotsam and jetsam of a city. An osprey sails overhead. A black skimmer flies just above the water, its long red toucan beak leaving a slim and precise trail on the surface.

The resin of bayberry bruises the air when I crush a leaf in my fingers. The shrubs' branches are crowded with waxy blue berries. Tart autumn olives are ripe, bright scarlet skins flecked with silver. Spangled in their fretwork of slim leaves, small white asters are beginning to bloom. The ivy that twines up the dry reeds is turning crimson. The season tilts.

We take a day's break beyond the borders of the city and drive out to the beautiful North Fork, as far from Brooklyn as we can get while remaining on Long Island. The blue lasts as far as we can see, transparent blue water meeting clear blue sky. One hundred miles northeast of home it is cooler by several degrees, the season a week or two ahead, lapped by the Atlantic breeze. We have driven through fields of late Queen Anne's lace, yellow streamers of solidago, and white mounds of starry asters in the fields and road-sides. Waves break cleanly onto sand cobbled with pebbles and transparently

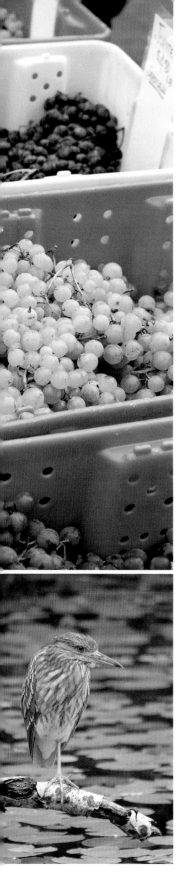

washed shells. Our picnic spread on the beach tastes better than a story—cucumbers and salt, thin ham and a baguette, and local North Fork wine. There is longing in my husband's green eyes, and I know that the sea is calling him. He lived for a decade in it. We drive back, our approach to the city slowing as traffic increases and the silhouettes of the mass of stalled cars ahead begin to halo in the bright, sinking sun.

In the dusk of midweek Brooklyn, we sit on the grassy hill at Pier 1 and look far out toward the Statue of Liberty and the Staten Island ferries that cross the harbor every thirty minutes in their rush hour. We sip cold riesling that turns golden in the glasses as the sun loses its grip on the skyline, throwing us into the cold shadow of skyscrapers.

We shiver. And that feels good.

Market Fresh

Concord Grape Granita

Concords are grapes with personality. Here the musky essence of the fruit is captured in a simple, crackling glassful of scented ice.

⫷ MAKES 3 CUPS (720 ML) ⫸

6 cups (900 g) Concord grapes	1 tablespoon fresh lemon juice

Crush the fruit lightly and heat with ⅓ cup (80 g) of water in a covered saucepan. Simmer gently for 10 minutes until the grapes have exuded much of their juice. Strain the liquid through a sieve into a bowl, mashing the grapes lightly to extract as much juice as possible. You should have about 2 cups (480 ml).

Add the lemon juice. Transfer the juice to a bowl and freeze. Check on it after 2 hours. As soon as it begins to freeze, scratch the frozen part free, into the unset liquid. Check and scratch every hour. The more often you scratch, the better the crystals will be.

Serve in small glasses.

Evenings have an edge as September progresses. The fire on the terrace is a welcome, warm glow as we eat our supper.

Early Fall Fish Cooked Over Coals

Whole fish cooked on the coals when the fennel on the terrace is in bloom and beginning to set young green seed is in tune with the cooling season. A sparkling fresh, bright-eyed branzino or a clutch of sardines, laid over sweet fennel branches and stuffed with nothing more than a lemon slice or two, comes close to perfection.

Choose the best fish you can find. The eyes should be bright. Any hint of a fishy smell is a hint too far. Skip.

≪ SERVES TWO ≫

1 fish, about 1½ pounds (680 g) per person, or 3 to 4 sardines each	Fennel fronds
	Olive oil
	Salt
Lime or lemon slices	Lime or lemon wedges, for serving

Have the fish gutted and scaled but left intact. Put two thin slices of lime or lemon in the cavity with a frond of fennel and a pinch of salt. Oil and salt the skin. Lay the fish about 4 inches above ashed-over coals and turn just once, cooking each side for roughly 12 minutes if the fire is not too hot. When the skin is blistering and turning brown and the head and eyes have turned opaque the fish is done. Remove to a platter and serve with fresh lime or lemon wedges.

Warm Potato Salad

I love astringent potato salads. The sorrel growing in a bucket on the roof above our heads is achingly sour and a perfect wake-up call for warm, mealy potatoes.

≪ SERVES TWO ≫

Pinch of salt	¼ cup (60 ml) extra-virgin olive oil
Pinch of sugar	
1 tablespoon fresh lemon juice	6 small to medium potatoes, boiled until tender, skins on
Freshly ground black pepper	2 cups (40 g) sorrel leaves, pulled from the midrib

In a small bowl, whisk the salt and sugar in the lemon juice to dissolve. Add pepper to taste. Whisk in the olive oil. In a medium bowl, put the still-hot potatoes and the sorrel leaves. Pour the vinaigrette over and toss. The sorrel will wilt on the hot potatoes and turn that unprepossessing khaki color. Taste for seasoning and add more salt and pepper if necessary.

THE
SEPTEMBER
TERRACE

For the first time in months the sliding door to the terrace is kept open again day and night and the air conditioner holds its breath after a summer-long racket. Suddenly, we can hear again. We had forgotten bird calls. A cardinal's alarm recalls me to the season. Sitting inside, I hear the high skree of the tiny American kestrel as it hunts the pigeon roosts in the crags of the hospital building that looms above our block. On the analog TV aerial across the road the little raptor pecks delicately at its dinner in icy disregard of its bombardment by a couple of enraged mockingbirds.

The tired flowers are granted a reprieve. The English roses regain their cabbage flounces. Munstead Wood swells deep red, three shades darker than its summer scarlet and now retains its voluptuous scent. Impossibly, the Etoile Violette blooms for a third time, after a late August trim. I love this plant.

Among the canes of the New Dawn, mute since spring, grows a self-seeded autumn-blooming clematis—*Clematis virginiana*. Irrepressible, it is sometimes considered a pest because of its promiscuity, but I value its delayed sprays of white blossom in very tight quarters. It is now tangled in the upper reaches of the leggy rose and covered with sprays of lightly fragrant white flowers. Above it in the porcelain blue President Obama's five-strong aerial cavalcade chops its way towards Manhattan, splitting the perfect air.

The fennel's yellow umbels are turning green with seed. The leaves of the remaining summer savory are rusty and it is shedding its own minute seeds dangerously. I gather as much as possible to prevent the terrace from being overwhelmed by its offspring in the spring. Chives are over a foot long and I cut handfuls of them to turn into evergreen oil to live in the fridge through the barren, chiveless months. Slathered on a midwinter baguette with some bresaola or a soft egg, it makes summer jump back to life.

Fall flowers start to bloom. Hardy begonias bear pendant pink and white petals around yellow pom-pom centers. Japanese anemones lean toward the light on elegant stems. The white wings of night-scented Abyssinian gladiolus glow in the earlier dark.

On a sunny, bright day the rare but unmistakable sound of ripping silk catapults me outside. An F-16 tears across the sky. The association of blue September with the fighter jets causes my skin to prickle. For a week after that terrible day in 2001 they patrolled the empty skies, too late. I don't know why it flies by this day, but it seems unkind to New Yorkers, who freeze, and look skywards. On the anniversary the twin beams of light from Manhattan travel so high into the night sky that we see them from where we sit eating dinner on the terrace, the stone table now cold to the touch in a night that turns chilly.

Tornado warnings and severe weather crashing toward New York like a red and yellow wall on the radar send me to the roof to batten down the hatches. A warm afternoon becomes dark and purple and then silent before all hell breaks loose, ushered in by a cold blast as the mass storms towards us across the harbor. The fig is secure on the stone table. Our sunset deck chairs lean on the landing, safe from flight. As the canopies of oaks over the road corkscrew in the wind we remember that we live on a planet that roars.

The weather clears.

On the roof farm, accompanied by the cat, we sip sundowners after I plant the contents of my newly arrived Botanical Interests package: fava beans, peas, lettuce leaves, mustard, kale, and microgreens. I harvest the last handfuls of tomatoes, and pick doomed green ones that cannot ripen in the shorter days ahead for a dish of classic fried green tomatoes—crisp on the outside, tart and piping hot. From our chairs we look across the back lots and trees and rooftops ahead of us, across the harbor and see in the clean, compressed light layers of detail that we had forgotten on the far New Jersey shore, past the water and past the ferries and tugs and barges and yachts. Ellis Island is in focus, the red brick of its buildings discernible beneath its cupolas against each twilight's reddening sun.

By the end of September the roof farm's greens are lush, and I have been picking them every night for peppery and delicate salads. The days have grown noticeably shorter and the sun sets further south of west each evening, now over the domes of old trees on nearby Governor's Island, and then passing our view's foreground of post-Panamax gantry cranes in Red Hook, and then the far off ones in Elizabeth, New Jersey, looking like dinosaurs come to the water to drink, long necks stretching from great bodies, moving in a creaking herd behind Lady Liberty.

Soon we think about taking sweaters up with us, and we drink our cocktails a little faster, and see through the skylights of the apartment the glow of warm, welcome light.

Chive Oil

This chive oil is wonderful spread on toast beneath a poached egg, or when used for basting roasting pork. (The yield will vary based on the size of the bunch of chives.) To sterilize the jar for this recipe, place it on the middle rack in a preheated 300°F (150°C) oven for 20 minutes, then remove with tongs and allow to cool before filling.

MAKES ABOUT 2 CUPS (480 ML)

1 large bunch fresh chives

Extra-virgin olive oil

Chop the chives finely and place them in a measuring cup. Pour an equal amount of oil into a blender and add the chives. Blend until smooth. Push the oil through a sieve into a bowl, to remove the fibers of the chives. Pour the bright green oil into a sterilized jar and store it in the refrigerator. It will keep for up to 4 months or more. *Do not store the oil at room temperature*, or you are inviting botulism (this goes for any oil infused with fresh herbs or garlic).

Fried Green Tomatoes

Piping hot, these tart, crisp tomatoes have lusciously soft insides, bursting with juice. They must be eaten as soon as they slide out of the pan.

SERVES TWO AS A MAIN COURSE

¼ cup (30 g) flour

Salt

Freshly ground black pepper

4 green tomatoes, sliced thick

¼ cup (60 ml) olive oil

Toast, for serving (optional)

Egg, poached, for serving (optional)

Sprinkle the flour onto a plate. Season it with salt and pepper. Dip the tomatoes in the flour, dusting both sides. In a large saucepan over medium-high heat, heat the oil. Add the tomato slices to the pan, about 4 at a time. Cook until golden on one side and oozing juice. Turn. Cook another 2 to 3 minutes until tender. Turn the tomatoes onto a piece of thick, good, toasted bread on a warmed plate. Eat on your lap while watching *Fried Green Tomatoes*. If you want to go all-out, top with a poached egg.

SEPTEMBER MENU

For me, September means bouillabaisse, a cool weather ritual. *Bagna càuda*, preceding the fish soup with its own anchovy base simmering over an open flame, is an opportunity to show off and to enjoy beautiful, raw vegetables, and to crowd around a communal dipping pot. The last plums of the year make a light end to a rich dinner.

early fall dinner

Transatlantic Cocktail

Bagna Càuda

Bouillabaisse

Poached Plums in Red Wine

Transatlantic Cocktail

This cocktail, born in our little apartment, is characterized by the marzipan fragrance of foraged serviceberries in Calvados. The infusion is versatile in a mixed drink, or sipped as a liqueur after dinner.

Why Transatlantic? American serviceberries, Italian prosecco, and Calvados from Normandy. Yes, this is a drink with a footprint.

≪ MAKES ONE DRINK ≫

1 ounce (2 tablespoons) serviceberry-infused Calvados (see page 107)   Chilled prosecco

Pour the Calvados into a flute or coupe and top with prosecco.

Bagna Càuda

A crowd-pleasing appetizer and also a satisfying stand-alone lunch or supper. The bubbling oil matches cold-weather thoughts. The bright vegetables are beautiful and their crisp rawness preserves all their vitamins and minerals. Their crunch is a perfect vehicle for melted anchovies and soft garlic.

If you don't have dishes that rest on trivets over candles, a small fondue pot or even a very small, heat-retaining cast iron pot will work—as long as you eat the *bagna càuda* as soon as it arrives at the table. It must stay very hot. For six people you may want two little pots, so divide the bath between them once cooked on the stove.

I recommend a piece of bread to catch any drips that fall between the pot and the mouth. Bread in one hand, vegetable in the other, poised over the bread, in and out of the pot.

Use as many vegetables as you can—at least five, for variety, planning on about a cup, total, per person. Divide them among several bowls on the table, for easy reach.

⟪ SERVES SIX ⟫

FOR THE WARM BATH

1 cup (240 ml) extra-virgin olive oil

10 anchovy fillets

8 cloves garlic, finely sliced

FOR DIPPING

Carrots, peeled and cut into spears

Beetroot, peeled and cut into thick batons

Belgian endive, separated into individual leaves

Sweet peppers, sliced into wide strips

Scallions, cleaned and trimmed

Cauliflower, broken into florets

Turnip, peeled and sliced into batons

Broccoli, cut into florets and stems peeled and sliced

Green beans or wax beans, trimmed

Radishes, tops retained as handles but tailed and then sliced in half

In a small saucepan, combine the oil, anchovies, and garlic. Bring the mixture to a simmer over high heat, then immediately reduce the heat to very low, or the garlic will cook too quickly, or, worse, burn and become bitter. Cook at a bare simmer for 10 to 15 minutes, until the garlic is confit-soft and the anchovies have melted into the oil. You can help them disintegrate by stirring them occasionally with a fork.

To serve, transfer the *bagna càuda* to a mini fondue pot or bring to the table and park the pot on a heatproof mat or wooden board. Dip the vegetables in the warm oil, catching a little of the anchovy mixture with each dip. My friend Mimi and I usually fight over the last caramelized morsels in the bottom of the dish.

Bouillabaisse

The memory of the best bouillabaisse I ever ate forms the palate reference for this recipe. Its source was unlikely—an Italian restaurant in Cape Town called La Vita, since expired, in the deeply suburban Dean Street Arcade. The soup was a rich orange, with Cape spiny lobsters bristling from it, and with it was served the most delicious hot-from-the-oven crusty white bread that I have ever eaten. My mother took me there after school, sometimes, and I sat in my horrible blue uniform dunking bread and sipping soup, perfectly happy and free and forgetting about my utter inability to grasp algebra.

No two sources will agree on what constitutes real bouillabaisse. Read Elizabeth David on the subject, in *French Provincial Cooking*. Mine is not authentic, but it is authentically mine.

If you can find them, and in New York we can, buy rouget—red mullet—the highly perishable but wonderful little red Mediterranean fish which are an excellent base for the soup. I also use branzino (also called European seabass), and other fine, white-fleshed fish. Avoid oily fish, such as sardines, mackerel, or bluefish. *Note: Please educate yourself about what fish are considered sustainable.*

You can make the stock the day before you plan to serve the bouillabaisse and finish the cooking just before dinner.

There are still good tomatoes available locally and this is as much a farewell to their summer redness as it is a greeting of a new, cool season.

Optional: If you are feeling rich, lobster is wonderful.

⪡ SERVES SIX ⪢

FOR THE STOCK

8 medium tomatoes

3 tablespoons olive oil

2 large onions, finely chopped

3 leeks, pale parts only, cleaned and thinly sliced

1 whole head garlic, cloves peeled and roughly chopped

2 bulbs fennel, chopped

2 carrots, chopped

3 stalks celery, thinly sliced

5 tablespoons (80 ml) tomato paste

6 bay leaves

12 sprigs thyme, tied in a bundle

1 bunch parsley

1 tablespoon whole black peppercorns

1 tablespoon sugar

1 teaspoon salt

6 small to medium white-fleshed ocean fish (about 1 to 1½ pounds / 455 to 680 g each), carcasses and heads only, fillets reserved

Shells and heads from 1½ pounds (680 g) of shrimp (if you can buy them head on), tails cleaned and reserved

1 bottle unwooded dry white wine or rosé

1 tablespoon sherry vinegar

FOR THE BOUILLABAISSE

Lobster tail and claws (optional)

2 pounds (910 g) small New Zealand cockles, rinsed well

Large pinch of saffron

3 tablespoons rouille (see below)

Make the stock: Slit the tops of the tomatoes and roast them on a tray for 40 minutes at 400°F (200°C) until they start to blacken and ooze juice. Cool, and remove their skins. Scrape up their juice and reserve.

Heat the oil in a large stockpot. Add the onions, leeks, and garlic, stir, and sauté gently for about 10 patient minutes on medium heat, until translucent and beginning to take golden color. Add all the other vegetables including the tomatoes and their collected juice and pan scrapings, and cook another 5 minutes, stirring from time to time.

Increase the heat, add the tomato paste, and stir again. Cook for a couple of minutes to let it caramelize a little.

Add the herbs, peppercorns, sugar, and salt.

Add the fish carcasses and the shrimp shells (if you have a lobster, add its carapace and legs, chopped in quarters, at this point—reserve the meat and claws). Pour in the bottle of wine and add about 6 cups (1.5 L) of water. The fish should be submerged. If not, add some more water.

Increase the heat and bring to a boil. Reduce immediately to a steady simmer (lots of steam, surface barely shaking, very small bubbles) and skim off any foam that rises. Cook for an hour and then turn off the heat. Add the vinegar.

When it has cooled a little, strain the stock in stages into a large bowl, pressing hard to get as much good-tasting juice as possible through the strainer. Pick out 3 cups of solids from the strainer: vegetables, as well as pieces of fish (without bones).

In a blender, puree these solids with a little of the stock until very smooth. Pour through the strainer again, back into the large bowl of stock. This gives your bouillabaisse the character that makes it memorable. Return the stock to the pot, heat to a boil once more, and reduce gently by one-quarter. This concentrates the flavor. Taste. Adjust the seasoning.

The stock is now ready to use. (You may chill it until you need it. Finishing the bouillabaisse will take about 15 minutes, once the stock is back at room temperature.)

Make the bouillabaisse: Remove the reserved prepared fish and shellfish from the fridge.

When the stock has begun to simmer, add the saffron and the reserved shrimp tails. After a minute, add the reserved fish fillets. Do this gradually as some of the heat will leave the stock as the cool fish goes in. Turn up the heat if necessary. If you have lobster, add it now.

When the liquid once again reaches a simmer, add the cockles. Cover the pot. As soon as the cockles have opened, the bouillabaisse is ready, about 1 to 3 minutes. Discard any cockles that do not open.

Stir the rouille gently into the pot, off the heat. (If the mixture is boiling, the egg in the rouille will cook and curdle.)

Serve in wide bowls, giving everyone a bit of everything. Dunk in some bread. Slather rouille on the bread. Drink wine. Be very happy to be eating this with people you like.

Rouille

Rouille is aioli with even more attitude.

This can be prepared well in advance. I prefer mayonnaise made with an unscented oil, such as canola or sunflower, rather than an extra-virgin olive oil, which, while wonderful in its own right, overpowers the idea of what a mayonnaise should be, for me.

≪ MAKES ABOUT 2 CUPS (480 ML) ≫

4 cloves garlic, peeled

¼ teaspoon salt

2 egg yolks, at room temperature

1 cup (240 ml) canola or sunflower oil

Pinch of saffron, soaked in 1 teaspoon water

½ teaspoon cayenne

1 tablespoon white wine vinegar or fresh lemon juice

On a chopping board, crush the garlic with the blade of a big knife. Work the salt into the garlic until it forms a paste. In a bowl, whisk the egg yolks. Slowly add half the oil in a very, very thin, steady stream. Beat or whisk continuously with the other hand, working in small amounts of the oil until it has disappeared, before adding more. When half of the oil has been added, stop whisking and add the garlic paste, saffron, cayenne, and vinegar or lemon juice. Resume adding the oil, beating steadily until the rouille has reached a very thick mayonnaise consistency. Transfer to a serving bowl and refrigerate.

If the sauce separates or does not emulsify, start in a clean bowl with a fresh egg yolk, and pour the flopped mixture very slowly into it, whisking steadily.

Poached Plums in Red Wine

Give me a fruit, and chances are, I will try to poach it.

Plums become surprisingly complex when cooked, turning from frankly sweet into something more interesting. Be very gentle, as they fall apart if boiled. If you do overcook them, fold them, cooled, into the Greek yogurt for a plum fool, and pretend you meant to do that all along. Alternatively, do what I did once by accident and now repeat on purpose: transfer the cooked pulp—without the stones—to a sterilized jar and keep in the fridge. They are now a versatile compôte, to be eaten with any kind of pork dish (see page 202).

⟪ SERVES SIX ⟫

6 red plums

2 cups (480 ml) red wine

3 tablespoons brown sugar

1 vanilla bean

1½ cups (360 ml) strained Greek yogurt

Place the plums with the wine, sugar, and vanilla bean in a saucepan and turn up the heat. Cover until the liquid reaches a boil. Immediately reduce the heat and simmer, covered, for 5 minutes. Remove the lid and continue to poach for another 10 minutes until tender. Remove the plums to a serving dish. Slit the vanilla bean in half lengthwise and scrape out the seeds, returning them to the wine. Over higher heat, reduce the wine until almost syrupy, and pour it over the plums. Eat cool, with a side of the creamy, unsweetened yogurt.

OCTOBER

Back in Pelham Bay Park in the Bronx, at the opposite end of the year, we spend an afternoon among trees and falling leaves and chickadees. I find spicebush berries and collect them for the cookies and the bourbon which they infuse with their lemon zest scent. The woods are thick with leaves and all interest lies upwards, now, and not at our feet, as it does in spring. Sassafras is flat yellow in thickets crowding the woodland path, and every oak is colored to temperatures of blood. The smooth cordgrass feathering the shoreline is pale, frayed straw. Treed islands float, reflected in the water's mirror surface. A man and a boy drift in a canoe, their life vests bright yellow against the autumn wall of trees on the shore beyond.

In Brooklyn, a long walk rising and falling among the hills and vales of Green-Wood reveals clusters of maitake (or hen of the woods) mushrooms, growing on the woody roots of giant beeches and soaring oaks still covered in rich green leaf. I collect them and fill a paper bag that becomes a significant weight as we walk. Beside a grassy path the unmistakable lavender caps of blewits rise just above the damp surface. I cut their stalks and add the pretty mushrooms to our stash. Large, nervous flocks of migrating northern flickers feed in the grass before rising up into the trees at my approach.

The first furred quinces arrive at the farmers' market, yellow and slightly bruised. I choose very small ones, which smell, as they ought to, of the sweetest apples. They will be dessert, roasted with juniper. I buy Honeycrisp apples and find elusive muscat grapes on Court Street. Supper shapes up. I carry my shopping home to the dark apartment where the warm lamplight reveals a sleeping cat and a terrace filled with quiet, cold plants above which, much later, several flights of geese pass, flying south.

Shorter days and longer nights signal our transition to daytime picnics, cold and brisk, when sitting in the sun becomes the pleasure we had half forgotten.

Halloween and its sense of otherness creep closer. Chrysanthemums and frilled kale are joined on stoop steps by jack-o'-lanterns and furry spiders.

Estorbo sits in the gutter at the edge of the terrace above the annual children's parade and looks like a staged cat, ready to fly.

I pick an eccentric posy from the terrace to take to friends for dinner. Strawberries on long stems, blue plectranthus, parsley, thyme, a spray of Mexican cherry tomatoes. After a very good meal, filled with roast rack of lamb and good red wine and excellent cheese that really did lie down and cry, we leave the Flatiron District at 11:30 and decide to walk back to Brooklyn.

Down Broadway, past the clubs, the lines, the very short skirts and very high heels, past bags of trash on sidewalks waiting for pickup, past garbage trucks collecting the contents of street trash cans posted at every corner, down past Spring Street, a look left to see the red awning of Balthazar and its own clutch of suited patrons in the yellow lamplight, on past Grand Street, Broadway quiet now, no clubs on the main drag, crossing Canal, all shut up, no Midwestern tourists buying knockoffs from dark West Africans, past Federal Plaza where we had our interview for Vincent's green card, on to City Hall where the irrigation system in the lawn has sprung two huge leaks that pour straight up and over the sidewalk, past the sign in the grass saying Passive Recreation Only No Team Sports, across the park and onto Brooklyn Bridge, empty now, past midnight, just a few walkers and cyclists heaving up the incline, the Frank Gehry building on the right, the Woolworth behind us in uplit ornate stone and green copper, a cool breeze but not cold with the walking. The cables of the bridge an orderly and exact beauty, the flag on the far side flapping, Manhattan's lying limp. Walking above the traffic where three cars are snarled in a rear-ender with police lights flashing and buckled bonnet and broken glass, a girl leaning over the balustrade from the boardwalk to see what is happening in this exciting New York. A seagull flying by, down toward the harbor, wings in spotlit white, the yellow lights of Staten Island making it seem a familiar town, just across the water. The temperature shows 63°F/17°C on the Watchtower building, and we walk down into Brooklyn past Cadman Plaza under the plane trees and into Brooklyn Heights, following Vince's running route, turning to his rhythm, on dark streets not of my habit, and walking down Henry, the last few blocks on tiptoe as my shoes unused to walking so far bite into my heels, stopping at the corner deli to buy cat food for the cat's emergency breakfast, seeing the Arabic owner giving the local addict his free sandwich for the night, the old man bent double and permanently plugged into headphones. We cross Atlantic, past the bar on Henry where lights and voices spill onto the sidewalk while apartments sleep above guarded by fire escapes, turning up to the townhouse steps, climbing the stairs, smelling the skunk of pot on the first floor, hearing the cat start to yell as we hit the second, key in lock, open door, home at 1:00 A.M.

Forager's Boeuf Bourguignon

The best boeuf bourguignon I've ever eaten was at Les Halles on Park Avenue for Anthony Bourdain's fiftieth birthday bash and book launch.

Bourdain's use of the weirdly named "chicken steak," a cut of chuck with a seam of fatty gristle running down the center, revolutionized my own recipe. Chicken steak is also called flatiron steak, paleron, and plain old chuck. But that seam in the middle defines it.

Earthy with freshly gathered hen-of-the-woods (maitake) mushrooms, fragrant with terrace-grown herbs, and sweet with carrots and onions, this is sloppy, happy fall food and is even better the next day, after chilling overnight.

❮❮ SERVES SIX ❯❯

3 ½ pounds (1.6 kg) chicken steak, cubed

Salt and freshly ground black pepper

4 strips fatty bacon or pancetta

2 tablespoons butter

3 onions, thinly sliced

2 tablespoons flour

1 bottle of red wine

3 large carrots, peeled and cut into 1 ½-inch (4-cm) sections (halve any thick pieces)

6 cloves garlic, slightly squashed

8 parsley stalks with leaves

10 sprigs thyme

3 bay leaves

3 cups (290 g) hen of the wood, in bite-size pieces

Baguette, for serving

Season the cubed beef with salt and pepper. In a heavy pot, cook the bacon over medium heat until the fat renders. Remove the bacon and set it aside. Increase the heat to high. In small batches, brown the seasoned beef in the rendered bacon fat. Remove the browned meat and set it aside in a bowl.

Reduce the heat and add the butter. When it foams, add the onions. Stir, then cover and sweat the onions for 5 minutes. Remove the lid and sauté for 10 minutes more, or until the onions are pale golden. Sprinkle the flour over the onions, stir again, and cook for a couple of minutes. Pour the wine over the onions and stir like mad to scrape up the *fond* (the delicious brown stuff stuck to the bottom of the pan). Return the meat to the pot and add the carrots, garlic, parsley, thyme, and bay leaves. Bring to a boil, then reduce the heat to keep the mixture at a gentle simmer. Cook for 1 hour, covered, stirring every now and then. Add the mushrooms. Cook for another 1 ¼ hours, uncovered, then taste and add salt and pepper as necessary. Test the meat with a fork; it should be fall-apart tender.

To serve, ladle the stew into bowls and set a hot-from-the-oven baguette (or two) in the middle of the table, ready to be torn apart by hungry hands.

THE {OCTOBER TERRACE

Spotless days turn inside out so that September roars away like a fiend, sweeping October in on wings of water.

Heeding wind gust warnings ahead of the outer bands of an approaching hurricane, I heave the fig down onto the stone table to prevent toppling. The wind throws the Iceberg rose onto the terrace, breaking its supports.

The gale pulls and tears and subsides and then rises to a shuddering pitch again, whistling, heaving, threatening. We are a creaking ship in a storm at sea. It begins to hail. Soon it rains, really, really hard, water sluicing through the gutters and down to the street.

The rain ends the next afternoon and the clouds open to admit the western sun. The silver roofs across the road turn gold and within seconds a rainbow materializes in the east, spanning Brooklyn from north to south, filling our horizon. The leaves of the fig and the strawberries are shredded.

And then the seamless blue days arrive. The air is electric. Every day the Vs of geese pass, southerning. Every evening the old brick hospital building that dwarfs our block lights up as though fired from within.

On the roof the dwarf kale and tender pea shoots and mesclun and mustard sown in the low troughs and pots empty of eggplant and pole tomatoes give us daily bowls of salad. Perhaps, in a former life, I was a rabbit: these pools of green leaves make me very happy. I collect the last branches of indefatigable cherry tomatoes.

Summer savory is drying in the low oven, the leaves and seeds remaining powerfully fragrant for months. I add them to goulashes and sprinkle them over wild mushroom pizzas, but never manage to use them all before the new season starts. The kitchen smells deliciously of sweet fern syrup on the stove. The apartment is warm, and for the first time in as long as I can remember that is a good thing.

I hear geese calling again in the night sky. It is a high, heartsore sound. The sound of seasons turning, countries calling, homes remembered, life passing. The sound of being left behind, and the desire to follow.

OCTOBER MENU

I was born at the end of October in the southern hemisphere. It is late springtime in South Africa, a month of wildflowers in ditches and fields and mountains. I miss that spring, but up here, eight thousand miles away in the north, I am happy to be breathing the fresh, dry air of a leaf-turning fall whose beauty I knew only from books. There is something about the quality of the light in both places, in this month, which is similar. A transparency, a sense of yearning that belongs to the months that touch each side of winter.

Comptonia Cocktail

Sweet fern is *Comptonia peregrina*. It has fragrant, hay-scented leaves that smell like summer. A nip of bourbon infused with the sweet fern and topped with sparkling wine, preferably sipped on a cold roof, after a long walk, with a good sunset, is my idea of October perfection.

⟪ MAKES ONE COCKTAIL ⟫

1 ounces (1 tablespoon) sweet fern bourbon (see Note)	Chilled cava

Pour 1 ounce of sweet fern bourbon into a flute and top with chilled cava.

Note: To make your own sweet fern bourbon, cover sweet fern leaves with 17 ounces (500 ml) bourbon in a big jar, and add ½ cup (100 g) sugar. Seal and allow to infuse for two months before straining and decanting.

birthday dinner with friends

Comptonia Cocktail

Smoked Trout Sambal with Watercress Salad

Brown Bread

Ouma's Spicy Lamb Shanks

Quinces Roast with Juniper

Smoked Trout Sambal with Watercress Salad

Some of the best influences on South African cooking came from the Indian Ocean rim, brought to the country with Southeast Asian slaves when the Dutch and then British exerted colonial control over seventeenth-, eighteenth-, and nineteenth-century South Africa.

In Cape Town this smoked fish sambal would be made with *snoek* (*Thyrsites atun*), a fish local to southern Atlantic waters and resembling a barracuda—long, silver, and pointy. Its oily flesh is perfect for smoking and flakes easily from the big bones. In New York, I use smoked trout, or mackerel. The sambal is best eaten within a couple of hours of preparation, while the raw onion is still fresh. If I were being true to tradition, the fish and onion would be pounded in a mortar until fine and resembling more of a paste. I prefer flakes.

Leftover sambal makes excellent potted fish for a picnic. Simply pack it quite tightly into a ramekin and pour melted butter over it. Chill, and it's ready to go.

‹‹ SERVES SIX ››

FOR THE SMOKED TROUT SAMBAL

4 smoked trout fillets (about 1 pound / 455 g)

1 medium onion (about ⅔ cup / 110 g), chopped very finely

2 teaspoons grated fresh ginger

Juice of 2 lemons

½ hot chile, sliced very thinly in rounds

Freshly ground black pepper

FOR THE WATERCRESS SALAD

1 farmers' market fresh apple, cored

Fresh lemon juice

2 bunches watercress, (5 loose cups / 170 g)

Extra-virgin olive oil

Salt

Butter, for serving

Brown Bread, for serving (see opposite page)

Make the sambal: Pull the skin from the fish fillets and discard. Using two forks, flake the flesh, carefully removing every bone you see. Now shred the trout more finely. Check for bones again.

In a bowl, mix the onion and ginger with the fish. Add enough lemon juice to moisten. Mix in the chile, and taste for spice levels and a good sour-salty balance. Add more lemon juice if you like. Finish with plenty of pepper.

Make the watercress salad: Cut the apple into very thin slices. Sprinkle some lemon juice over them. Heap the watercress in a salad bowl or on a flat plate and shake some olive oil over it. Sprinkle some lemon juice over that, and finish with a light dusting of salt. Top or surround with the apple.

To serve, transfer the fish to a pretty bowl and allow everyone to help themselves with a spoon. Butter slices of brown bread, press the fish onto it, and take a bite. Follow with a sprig of watercress and a crunchy apple slice.

Brown Bread

Walk into any supermarket or bakery, any food shop, any corner café (the South African equivalent of a deli or bodega), and you will find variations of this moist brown bread. These dense—but not heavy—nutty-tasting loaves are impossible to find beyond South Africa, and must be made at home.

A slice of this bread is the perfect vehicle for some grated cheddar with a dollop of chutney, or butter and jam at breakfast, or for piles of the smoky, salty sambal, pressed into its buttered surface.

《 MAKES 1 LOAF 》

1 tablespoon sugar	¾ pound (340 g) whole-wheat flour	¼ teaspoon salt	3 tablespoons currants, raisins, or sunflower seeds
2 teaspoons yeast			

Preheat the oven to 350°F (180°C). Grease a loaf pan well.

Stir the sugar and yeast into 1 cup (240 ml) of water and leave to bubble. Mix the flour and salt together in a large bowl. When the yeast mixture is bubbly, pour it into the flour mixture and stir well with a wooden spoon. Add another ¾ cup (180 ml) of water and the currants, stirring to combine. Pour this loose, sticky dough into the prepared pan and bake for 40 to 50 minutes, or until a skewer inserted into the bread comes out clean. Turn the bread out of the pan—the loaf should sound hollow when tapped on the bottom—and allow to cool, wrapped loosely in a clean dishcloth.

Ouma's Spicy Lamb Shanks

When you stand with each of your feet on a different continent, you learn to live with a constant sense of longing for the other place. I lull the longing with food.

When I left South Africa for what was intended to be a six-month stay in the States my mother gave me a recipe book that she had written by hand, just for me, with all my favorite food in it, including Ouma's Spicy Lamb Shanks. My mother knew what I did not: that I wasn't coming back. I left her at the airport with tears streaming down her face. That is my great regret.

These lamb shanks are my grandmother Quez's recipe. Her name comes from the Xhosa word *khwezi*, meaning "star"—an unusual choice for a white child born in South Africa at the end of the nineteenth century. Her father was a transport rider, driving wagons between towns during the Anglo-Boer War, and he must have seen many stars every dark night.

I like to serve this stew—or tagine—with nothing more than a heaping bowl of steaming farro, cooked until tender, and into which I have stirred a tablespoon of butter. Incidentally, this is one dish not to prepare a day ahead, as so many stews are. The lamb shanks remain resolutely tough when reheated.

❮❮ SERVES SIX ❯❯

6 lamb shanks, each cut into 3 or 4 pieces	1 cup (175 g) prunes, soaked in hot water	1 ¼ teaspoons black pepper	¾ teaspoon cloves
Salt and freshly ground black pepper	1 cup (150 g) raisins, soaked in hot water	¾ teaspoon cinnamon	3 tablespoons plus 1 teaspoon red wine vinegar
¼ cup (30 g) flour	½ cup (100 g) sugar	¾ teaspoon allspice	¼ teaspoon salt

Preheat the oven to 350°F (180°C). Grease a casserole dish with a lid.

Season the lamb shanks with salt and pepper. Dust them with the flour, shaking off any excess. Place the shanks in the prepared casserole and cook, covered, until tender, about 2 hours.

In a saucepan over medium heat, combine the remaining ingredients with 1½ cups (360 ml) of water. Bring to a boil and then simmer for 5 minutes.

Remove the casserole from the oven and drain the fat that has accumulated (but save any brown juices). Add the fruit mixture, return to the oven, and cook another 30 minutes. Serve from the dish at table.

Quinces Roast with Juniper

In the Karoo at the end of summer in South Africa quinces line dusty farm roads. In the Cape they are planted as espaliered hedges on grand farms within low whitewashed walls. Their perfume is intense. It is like the sum of all the best apples you have ever tasted and some about which you may only have dreamed. A bowl of ripe quinces is one of the happiest things imaginable.

Cooked, they are acquiescent and surprising, turning garnet and firm in a slow syrup, or pale and soft when baked in a low oven. Roasted, they are chewy on the outside, creamy in the middle. They partner well with pork, lamb, and game and are wonderful as dessert. Chewed while still fleshy, the juniper berries are a sweet, seedy snack, with a pungency that suggests good gin.

⟨⟨ SERVES SIX ⟩⟩

6 small quinces, skins brushed to remove fuzz, cored, and halved

⅓ cup (65 g) sugar

8 juniper berries

Preheat the oven to 350°F (180°C).

Put the halved quinces in a flat baking dish with 1 cup (240 ml) water, the sugar, and the juniper berries. Roast them for 90 minutes. Baste occasionally and check on the pan syrup, adding water if it threatens to dry up.

It sounds suspiciously simple, but that's all they need. The fruit is a little tart but very soft, and the skins are pleasurably chewy with caramelized edges.

NOVEMBER

NEW YORK IN NOVEMBER

Average temperatures: 54°F / 41°F (12°C / 5°C)

These November days of trees—hawthorn and oak, maple, zelkova, gingko and crab apple, linden, golden rain and pear, locust and beech, the contracting of the year, the intensifying light near each afternoon's end, stir an annual, visceral ache. The change of season is now profound and unstoppable. The weeks when russet and tawny autumn envelop the city are a steady progression toward an ideal of celebration, friends around dinner tables, golden light spilling onto cold sidewalks. Now I feel like a shy visitor in this northern hemisphere—inhabiting the weather and the season of stories told in books and countless movies—on chilled streets, past windows lit and warm in the late, dark afternoon. The clock has been turned back, and we are plunged into a winter of nights.

In The Ramble, the wooded and color-drenched heart of Central Park, an elderly man asks me how my eyesight is, and is that thing a raccoon, high up in that tree? I say no, it is probably a squirrel nest. Drey! we both exclaim in sudden unison. We part as friends, warning each other about suddenly falling branches after a recent snowfall on the still-leafed trees. People who work with trees call these Damoclean branches widow makers, their fall swift and impact final. The whine of a distant chainsaw is the sound of the park at work, clearing the damage. The paths are hidden completely beneath damp leaves. The air smells like humus and rain. A red cardinal freezes on a yellow branch.

Deep in the woods of Staten Island's High Rock Park we crush leaves underfoot on our way to a visit a cathedral of beeches whose size and nobility seem Gothic within the city. With my camera I lie beneath them, flat on my stomach in a carpet of leaves inches thick . . . I hear Vincent and our friend Frank Meuschke rustling somewhere nearby, each on his own mission—salamanders and mushrooms, respectively—but there is no one else in sight. We could be anywhere. Vince hums happily as he turns over a log and finds his vertebrate beneath.

A week later in Prospect Park's Midwood, the oldest and last piece of forest in Brooklyn, my feet skid on the layers of fallen brown oak leaves, piled deep. I am on another mushroom quest. An upright stump, a dead tree broken off at about twelve feet, is spiraled by young oysters. My heart leaps. A familiar log yields more mature fawn-capped specimens, which are cut and stashed in my paper bag. In the split seams of an enormous fallen tree enokis bristle, sticky and tan. I conjure recipes, plot Japanese broths.

At Borough Hall new apples and pears pour in. The first cold-sweet broccoli arrives. I swoop down on it like a starved deer. It bears no resemblance to its wan and ice-packed summer incarnation. Supper becomes bruschetta, the intensely cruciferous florets drizzled with anchovy and garlic.

In our neighborhood the stiff chrysanthemums and kale have been joined at front doors and in window boxes by winterberry and evergreen branches, bright gourds and sheaves of Indian corn, their rows of kernels a kaleidoscope arrested in the turning. Beside and behind them, windows glow like warm coals. In summer these houses remain opaque and removed, and the life within makes no impression. In these revealing times domestic life is exposed: a flatscreen TV and a couch, sitting in the blue light, every night, rooms with chandeliers and books, an old lady in a chair under a lamp, reading, people talking in the kitchen, backs to the window. A table set for supper.

It is Thanksgiving. In stores, fresh cranberries appear in stacked bags. Sweet potatoes are moved from their forgotten dusty heap to front row, center. Yellow cornmeal sells out. Canned pumpkin is restocked in the middle aisle. Butcher shops buzz with action. Everyone buys Brussels sprouts.

On the last Thursday of the month, I walk five deserted wintery blocks for last-minute shopping for our Thanksgiving dinner. I am in possession of a good, remarkably expensive ham, which belonged to an allegedly happy pig. We will sit down to eat in the evening, not at the traditional 4:00 P.M., when all I want is tea. The store is almost empty. Two girls check out with Brussels sprouts and sweet potatoes. Five young men prowl the aisles and confer frequently, stopping at what is left of the canned pumpkin. The cashiers are not sitting down to eat today. Outside there are few souls on the street, and there is no traffic. A man with shopping bags looks furtive, out alone on such a day. Couples standing in doorways are dressed up and holding covered plates, waiting to be let in. From many windows light streams hospitably; inside, tables are ready for the meal that the whole country shares. Tablecloths, plates, and people holding drinks. In one dining room a family sits down, an ancient lady with pale green hair, a middle aged man looking concerned and prodding a bowl with a fork, the old lady smiling happily. Another man adjusting the needle on a real record player, a child in the background.

I see two pizzas being delivered to an expensive front door. A woman is sipping a glass of white wine on a stoop, keeping her smoking friend company.

Two old men are slumped in wheelchairs under the dripping porch of the nursing home. The restaurant on the corner is closed, chairs on tables.

Walking back up the stairs of our building, I smell roasting marshmallows.

Market Fresh

Broccoli Bruschetta

In peak season it is possible to find broccoli still attached to its leaves, which are delicious. They look like miniature collard greens, with a serious, thick midrib. I cook them all on their own, like this. After a cold snap broccoli is addictively sweet. Substitute the florets or the peeled and sliced stems, if you can't find leaves.

❮❮ MAKES 4 PIECES ❯❯

¼ cup (60 ml) olive oil

3 cloves garlic, thinly sliced garlic

6 anchovy fillets

½ pound (225 g) broccoli leaves (or florets, or peeled stems sliced lengthwise)

Pinch of salt

Fresh lemon juice

Freshly ground black pepper

4 pieces whole wheat baguette or bread

1 clove garlic, peeled

Heat the oil gently in a small saucepan over medium-low heat. Add the garlic and anchovies and cook slowly for about 10 minutes, until the garlic is soft and the anchovies have dissolved.

Add ¼ inch (6 mm) of water to a pot, with the salt. Bring to a boil and add the broccoli. Cook, covered, until the broccoli can be pierced easily with the tip of a knife. Drain the broccoli in a colander and return it to the pot. Over medium heat, pour the anchovy mixture over the broccoli. Toss it all very well. Add a squeeze of lemon juice and top with plenty of pepper.

Meanwhile, you have been toasting bread. A peeled garlic clove lies ready to be rubbed over the hot bread as soon as it is toasted. Whip the bread out, rub the garlic over its surface, back and forth, pile on the broccoli, and eat at once.

THE NOVEMBER TERRACE

Even as the strawberries' leaves turn crimson their berries continue to sweeten, more than fulfilling their everbearing promise. The roses continue to bloom. In cool November, with the lower angle of the sun and the long black nights, the pulse of the opening flowers and ripening fruit slows to a contemplative rate that signals the approach of dormancy. A strawberry remains red for weeks without turning, a rosebud is perfect for days. Small floral dramas unfold in increments.

A modest pocket within the turning city, the terrace moves into its own autumn colors, adopting ochre in the forest grass and fulvous stripes in the leaves yellowing on the tall lily stalks whose potential for cold weather appeal I had not originally considered. The blueberry is ablaze with coppery orange and the fig leaves are lemon flags against the clear sky. The climbing roses mottle with blackspot, becoming ornamental as the season of diminishing returns forces a reconsideration of beauty.

I water the pots and see, when I step onto a chair to reach the faraway plants, the lights coming on in the apartments across the road, proof of life in the city of millions. The oak trees on the street are still fully leafed, their canopies glowing in the saturated light of late afternoon.

On the roof the ignored skeletons of the last holdout tomato and pepper plants must be dealt with and I make a clean sweep of all the pots. I stack the wire teepees and wedge them between pots against high winds. The bones of the farm show. In half the pots the mustards, peas, fava beans, kale, some radishes, and parsnip leaves are now the only visible green. My hands are freezing. So are my feet: habit sent me up the ladder barefoot, but the temperature is Arctic and after an hour in the late afternoon I can barely feel them.

In the bedroom the soft, deep snowdrift of the down comforter is spread for the first time since last winter, and the cat deigns to stay on it. We sleep with the window open, loving the contrast of the freezing air that drops from it and the luxurious warmth of our bed.

Ginger Ale Ham

The recipe and method have two parts: the slow-cooking, followed by a brief baking. Begin 24 hours before you wish to eat the ham.

A pickled or smoked pork shoulder is often called a picnic ham. The butt—a regular ham—is too large for this treatment.

I make this ham almost every year for Thanksgiving. My mother makes it for Christmas.

Cooking with ginger ale may seem bizarre, but you only live once. People who eat this pig never forget it: ginger ale pig may be a culinary abomination but it will make you long for more.

I have carried it on the subway, where passengers' noses twitched appreciatively in its direction, transported it in cabs, sliding around with it on the back seat, and served it at home. Accompanied by its fluffy mustard sauce it has made a grown man cry.

The process of slow-cooking the pork using a hot box method is low-fuss and easy on the gas bill.

❮❮ SERVES SIX TO TEN ❯❯

1 pickled or smoked pork shoulder with skin

1 tablespoon black peppercorns

8 bay leaves

10 whole cloves

20 juniper berries, crushed

8 cloves garlic, slightly squashed

1 onion, peeled and cut into quarters

1 carrot, halved

4 (1 L) bottles ginger ale

⅓ cup (20 g) whole, intact cloves

FOR THE RUB

¼ cup (30 g) dry, powdered mustard

½ cup (110 g) brown sugar

FOR THE SAUCE

2 egg yolks

1 tablespoon sugar

3 tablespoons prepared mustard (use dry powdered mustard mixed with equal parts water)

2 tablespoons vinegar

¼ teaspoon salt

1 tablespoon unsalted butter

½ cup (120 ml) heavy cream, whipped to soft mounds

Place the pork shoulder, shank end up, in a very large stockpot. Add the peppercorns, bay leaves, whole cloves, juniper berries, garlic, onion, carrot, and enough ginger ale to cover. If you don't have enough ginger ale, add water. The meat must be submerged.

Put the lid on, bring the liquid to a boil, and make sure it stays at a strong simmer for 30 minutes.

Now comes the fun part . . .

Prepare a bed for the pig. It needs to be very well insulated overnight or for at least 12 hours. I choose a corner on the floor, where the very full and heavy pot can be wedged without fear of toppling. I start with a feather cushion, protected with a cloth or towel in case anything spills. I rest the pot on top of the cushion, wrap three blankets or shawls or *kikois* right around the pot, put another on top, and top with a second cushion. I pack more cushions around the sides and top with a final blanket. If you happen to have a spare mink coat lying about, drape that over the top.

After 12 hours, unpack the pig. The pot should still be very hot. Lift the pot back onto the stove. (Bend at the knees!) Remove the shoulder carefully from the hot stock. Reserve 1 cup (240 ml) of the stock for immediate use; strain and freeze the rest for soup, stews, or beans.

Preheat the oven to 350°F (180°C).

Place the pork on a board, and cut and pull away the skin very carefully, leaving a good layer of fat beneath. Where the fat is more than ¼ inch (6 mm) thick, shave it off.

Using the knife tip, score the fat in parallel stripes and then again across those to create diamond shapes. Don't cut down to the meat or the fat will lift and peel away during baking.

At each intersection of the score lines, insert one whole clove.

Make the rub: Mix the powdered mustard and brown sugar in a small bowl. Pat and press enough of the mustard mixture to cover the scored fat.

Place the pork in a roasting pan with the reserved stock. Bake for about 40 minutes, patting some more of the mustard mixture over the pork while it is baking, as it tends to slide off in the heat as it melts and caramelizes. Drizzle the caramelizing cooking liquid over the pork every time you reapply the mustard mixture. You may have some mustard mixture left over.

When the shoulder is a glistening mahogany, after about 40 minutes, remove it from the oven and set aside to cool.

Make the sauce: Mix the egg yolks, sugar, mustard, vinegar, and salt with 1 tablespoon of water in a small bowl. Transfer the mixture to a small saucepan and heat very, very gently over very, very low heat. Whisk continuously as it thickens, for about 5 minutes. Remove the sauce from the heat when it becomes thick. Blend in the butter, whisking as it melts. When the sauce has cooled, add the whipped cream and stir thoroughly. Taste for salt. Transfer to a serving bowl and chill for at least 30 minutes.

Slice the ham and serve with a dollop of the sauce. My mouth waters as I write this.

NOVEMBER MENU

November is an auspicious month, leading up to one great culinary excess: Thanksgiving, that great, long meal. Everyone has their stock repertoire for it and I have developed mine, too (see page 196).

But here is a less loaded meal, viewed through a Thanksgiving lens and shared with friends who have not yet left town to celebrate with relatives around a big table. Vincent and I are immigrants, intimate orphans on this greatest traveling holiday of the year.

I employ what is left on the terrace: the mint on the sheltered gravel floor persists and is paired with citrus in a simple, North African–style salad. Fennel seeds are collected and perfume a slow-roasted pork belly. It fills the middle of leisurely dinner that starts with a warm and creamy cauliflower soup and ends with trembling panna cotta.

Thanksgiving Cocktail

Grand Marnier is one of the bluebloods of the liquor cabinet. Or liquor tray, in our case.

❮❮ MAKES ONE DRINK ❯❯

½ ounce (1 tablespoon) Grand Marnier   **Very cold Champagne**

For a very refined cocktail redolent of citrus, pour the Grand Marnier into a flute and top with Champagne.

holiday dinner

Thanksgiving Cocktail

Toasted Cumin Cauliflower Soup

Orange, Olive, and Chile Salad with Mint

Fennel-Roasted Pork Belly

Sweet Potatoes with Citrus

Panna Cotta with Bergamot-Infused Cranberries

Toasted Cumin Cauliflower Soup

Cauliflower seems very underrated. Try to pick one up at a farmers' market. It will generally possess more character and less bland liquid than the shrink-wrapped variety. The toasting of cumin adds warmth to the creamy soup and the dried lime a hint of Persia. If you can't find dried limes online or in person, substitute three strips of lemon zest, or two lime leaves.

《 SERVES SIX 》

2 tablespoons unsalted butter

1 head cauliflower, broken into florets

½ teaspoon ground cumin

¼ teaspoon powdered sumac, plus more for dusting

5 cups (1.2 L) chicken or vegetable stock, warmed

1 dried lime

1 tablespoon fresh lemon juice

Salt

¼ cup (60 ml) heavy cream

Freshly ground black pepper

In a large pot over medium-high heat, melt the butter. When it foams, add the florets and toss to coat. Sprinkle the cumin over. Toast, being careful not to scorch, until all the cauliflower florets have golden edges. Add the sumac and the warm stock. Add the dried lime. Pierce it in a couple of places. Bring the mixture to a simmer and cook until the cauliflower is tender. Add the lemon juice and season with salt to taste. Turn off the heat and allow to sit for 10 minutes. Remove and discard the dried lime. Puree the soup in batches. Return the pureed soup to the pot, add the cream, and bring back up to heat. Taste. Season with pepper, and serve hot with a light dusting of sumac.

Orange, Olive, and Chile Salad with Mint

I first tasted a salad like this at Café Gitane, a modest, resilient and perennially fashionable Algerian-French restaurant on Mulberry Street in Nolita. I was hooked.

Nothing could be more simple or surprising. Oil-cured olives are unapologetic, their succulence accompanied by a wallop of salt that is tempered by the sweet oranges. The fresh mint turns the salad into a bright bite before the rich pork to come.

⫷ SERVES SIX ⫸

6 oranges, suprêmed (see Note)

1 cup (135 g) oil-cured black olives, pitted

1 teaspoon hot chile flakes or Sriracha sauce

Freshly ground black pepper

1 tablespoon extra-virgin olive oil

12 fresh mint leaves

In a bowl, toss the orange segments with the olives, chile, and pepper and allow to sit for at least 1 hour in the refrigerator, covered. When you are ready to serve, stack the mint leaves on top of one another, roll them into a tube, and cut them into thin slices (this is called a "chiffonade"). Or just tear them up (this is called "tearing them up"). Arrange the orange salad in a bowl or plate and strew the mint across the top.

Note: To suprême an orange (or other citrus fruit), slice off both ends. Stand the orange on a cut end, then use a paring knife to cut away the skin and the pith. When the skin and pith have been removed, cut along the membranes between each segment of the fruit. Place the segments in a small bowl until needed.

Fennel-Roasted Pork Belly

Pork belly has a wonderful crackling-to-meat ratio and is rich. A little goes a long way. Because it is essentially self-basting you are left, after a three-hour roast, with a pig that melts in the mouth before the snap of crackle hits your teeth.

≪ SERVES SIX ≫

5 cloves garlic, peeled

Salt

2 tablespoons fennel seeds

Grated zest of 1 lemon

1 pork belly, about 4 ½ pounds (2 kg), skin slashed through the fat layer and across the width at 1-inch (2.5-cm) intervals

Freshly ground black pepper

Fennel branches or leaves

¼ cup (60 ml) fresh lemon juice

Pickled mustard, for serving (see opposite)

Preheat the oven to 400°F (200°C).

Using the flat of a large kitchen knife, crush the garlic cloves ¼ teaspoon salt until they form a paste. Add the fennel seeds and lemon zest and work them into the paste.

Push the garlic and fennel mixture into the slashes in the pork belly, avoiding the top of the skin. Push any garlic that lurks on the skin back into the slits, or it will burn. Rub the underside of the meat with any leftover garlic mixture. Season the skin with a little more salt and pepper. Spread the fennel stalks or leaves on the bottom of the roasting dish and place the belly on top to cover. Pour the lemon juice into the pan, taking care not to wet the pork belly skin; it will not crackle if wet. Add ½ cup (120 ml) of water.

Roast the belly for 3 hours, adding water to the pan if it looks dry.

When the pork is a rich brown and the skin has crackled, remove from the oven. Transfer the meat to a board or platter. After 10 minutes, slice it along the slashes. Serve with the pickled mustard or a plum compôte (see page 173).

Pickled Mustard

This is one of my kitchen staples. The inspiration for it comes from Momofuku Noodle Bar in the East Village, our favorite of David Chang's restaurants.

1 cup (80 g) mustard seeds

1½ cups (360 ml) apple cider vinegar

½ cup (100 g) sugar

1 tablespoon salt

Combine all the ingredients with 1½ cups (360 ml) of water in a small saucepan over medium heat. Cook at a bare simmer until the seeds are tender, adding more water if the mixture runs dry. Cool and store in sterilized glass jars (see page 165) in the fridge.

Fluffy Sweet Potatoes with Citrus

Sweet potatoes, or yams, as some people mistakenly call these orange-fleshed tubers, are quintessential winter fare. They are a homely but fragrant and soft partner for the pork, catching all its delicious juice. The citrus and the serious kick of pepper help counter its fat. Made in advance, this reheats very well over gentle heat.

≪ SERVES SIX ≫

6 sweet potatoes, peeled and cut into slices

1 cup (240 ml) fresh orange juice

1 tablespoon fresh lime juice

1 tablespoon maple syrup

2 tablespoons unsalted butter

½ teaspoon black pepper

Salt

Cook the potatoes in salted, boiling water until tender. Drain thoroughly. Coax them through a potato ricer into the pot in which they were cooked.

In a small saucepan, bring the orange juice to a boil and cook until reduced to ¼ cup (60 ml). Add the warm orange juice reduction, the lime juice, maple syrup, butter, and pepper to the sweet potato puree and set over low heat. Stir very well until the mixture is perfectly smooth and blended. Taste. Add salt. Cook a little longer, stirring, to reduce excess moisture, and serve hot.

Panna Cotta with Bergamot-Infused Cranberries

My love of desserts that jiggle makes me very fond of panna cotta. By varying the flavorings and the fruit sauces it is highly adaptable to the seasons. In summer I like it with white rum and fresh raspberries. But winter calls for something darker, and November means cranberries. You could make a fresh cranberry sauce, but I like the dried fruit, infused with bergamot tea and bourbon.

These can be made the day before you need them.

≪ SERVES SIX ≫

FOR THE PANNA COTTA

⅓ cup (80 ml) milk

1 (¼-ounce / 7-g) packet of gelatin

3 cups (720 ml) whipping cream

¼ cup (50 g) sugar

3 strips lemon zest, about ¼ inch by 3 inches (6 mm by 7.5 cm)

3 tablespoons bourbon

FOR THE BERGAMOT AND BOURBON-INFUSED CRANBERRIES

3 tablespoons bourbon

1 cup (240 ml) hot strong tea with bergamot (such as Earl Grey or Ahmad Afternoon Tea)

1 cup (120 g) dried cranberries

Make the panna cotta: Pour the milk into a small saucepan and bring to a simmer over medium heat. Turn off the flame and sprinkle the gelatin over the milk to soften. Stir thoroughly to dissolve.

In another saucepan over medium heat, heat 1½ cups (360 ml) of the cream, the sugar, and the lemon zest. Stir the mixture to dissolve the sugar. Bring the mixture to a brief boil, then immediately remove it from the heat. Scoop out the strips of zest. Add the warm milk and gelatin mixture to the hot cream and whisk very well to dissolve any stubborn gelatin lumps. Pour through a strainer into a bowl. Add the bourbon and stir. Allow the mixture to cool.

Whip the remaining 1½ cups (360 ml) of cream until thick. Mix gently into the cooled cream mixture.

Pour the cream into small, individual molds and chill for at least 3 hours.

Make the cranberries: Pour the bourbon and the hot tea over the cranberries and leave to infuse for at least 6 hours.

To serve, unmold each panna cotta by sliding a knife dipped in boiling water around the edges, and flipping onto a small plate. Sometimes it helps to dip the base of the mold for a split second in the hot water, too.

Serve each panna cotta with a spoonful of cranberries scattered around its feet.

DECEMBER

NEW YORK IN DECEMBER

Then it is December.

It is steadfastly dark at 4:00 P.M. and the nights are long. It is the first real month of winter.

The skies of these winter days are crystalline and blue and if there is a snow-fall every ugliness of the city is softened for some suspended hours beneath it. We contemplate the stark architecture of trees. Beneath their bare branches the city exhales plumes of steam from orange air vents. Fallen brown leaves still crunch underfoot and all growth seems withheld without doubt, but in Chinatown and in Cobble Hill, pale pink blossoms confuse passersby who think that The End has come: the vernal cherries are in spartan bloom.

As darkness draws in, windows light up and life pours from brownstones onto the brittle sidewalks where late afternoon footsteps ring between build-ings and each home is a beacon in the dark.

The migrants have arrived. On corners the Québécois tree sellers make a stand with their rows of firs. The Canadians have beards and woolen hats and unselfconscious plaid shirts and speak with ze accents from ze cold places up nors. Fresh-cut Douglas fir branches are sweet and resinous, and the smell of balsam carries across streets. Promise is in the air.

In the bare parks and snapping temperatures oyster mushrooms continue to evolve from pale pinheads to wide white fans on old logs and enokis bristle from thin fissures in fallen branches. I still carry mushrooms home for supper.

Just before midnight on New Year's Eve Vincent and I take a walk to the Promenade in falling snow, through Brooklyn Heights. Our blood still fizzes with our Champagne supper. We stand with our backs to New York Harbor and watch a party in a brownstone. Double bass, saxophone, a singer, and couples dancing in the warm light. Behind us people wrapped in coats and scarves gather under umbrellas, looking at the fairy-lit towers of downtown Manhattan across the black East River. From the southern end of the Prom-enade 1920s dance music comes drifting, as though we are dreaming. I think that someone has set up an old-fashioned gramophone. It is the sort of thing that will happen here.

We watch far-off fireworks, and turn home, walking past pairs of cops, out in force, obligingly taking pictures of tourists and turning a blind eye to celebratory Champagne corks popping as January and the new year begin.

The '20s dance music is coming out of a police cruiser parked at the end of the Promenade, lights blazing, music streaming to us from the powerful roof-mounted loud-hailer. We smile. Happy New Year, says the cop to us through his open window, from his seat inside.

Happy New Year, we say.

Mushroom Risotto

The oyster mushrooms of winter are generous, and this risotto is a staple December dish. To clean foraged oyster mushrooms submerge them completely in salty water. Cold-weather mushrooms are typically bug free, but I like to check. Dry them very well by pressing on them firmly with clean dish towels. They absorb a lot of water, like a sponge.

⟪ SERVES TWO, OR FOUR AS AN APPETIZER ⟫

3 tablespoons unsalted butter	1 cup (200 g) arborio rice	1 cup (100 g) finely grated Parmigiano Reggiano
4 cups (384 g) oyster mushrooms, cut into strips	½ cup (120 ml) dry white wine	Salt
2 tablespoons fresh lemon juice	3 cups (720 ml) hot mushroom, vegetable, or chicken stock	Freshly ground black pepper
2 shallots, finely chopped		

In a medium saucepan over medium-high heat, melt 2 tablespoons of the butter until it foams. Add the mushrooms and cover to allow them to sweat and exude water. Uncover and cook until the liquid dries up and the edges of the mushrooms begin to turn dark brown. Add 1 tablespoon of the lemon juice, stir, and cook until it has sizzled off. Remove the mushrooms to a bowl and lower the heat under the pan. Melt the remaining 1 tablespoon of butter and add the shallots. Cook gently until they are translucent. Add the rice and toast, stirring until it turns a chalky white. Turn up the heat and add the wine. Keep stirring until it has been absorbed. Add ½ cup (120 ml) of hot stock, and stir until it has been absorbed. Repeat. Add the mushrooms, and stir thoroughly. Keep adding gulps of hot stock, stirring between each addition.

After about 15 minutes of this, taste the rice. It must be firm, but not crunchy in the middle, either. When the rice is just cooked, usually after 20 to 25 minutes, add the last tablespoon of lemon juice, and stir. Add the cheese, and stir. Taste. Add the salt last. Season liberally with pepper. Turn the risotto into a warmed bowl, and eat at once. Risotto waits for no one.

THE DECEMBER TERRACE

The plants are hunkering down for a long cold stretch of months. Tough times. The leaves on the thyme plants on the sunny edge of the terrace have become leathery but their flavor remains strong. The water that collects in the copper bowl of the *braai* freezes solid.

The fig stands, gray arms skyward, a negation of the fruit of late summer and early fall, a barren contradiction of the bowls of sweetness that fed us for evenings in a row, making me think that it was possible, then, to have too many figs. Now it seems impossible that they could ever return.

On the roof farm the Italian kale withstands the wind and is cut to be eaten for chewy salads. The dwarf kale is in bloom, acid yellow against the chimney stacks and satellite dishes. The flowers snap with mustard and are wilted as a side dish for steak. Early in the month the peas still push out tender growth, relishing the cold. The cat skitters across the silvertop, flattening his ears and trying to duck the wind off the water.

The full moon rises northward, swung beyond its early summer alignment with the terrace, perfectly east and dead ahead. It is the pendulum whose position tells the time of year.

Despite the lack of change in the little garden, it is precisely this long, chilly, suspended rest that gives meaning to the other side of the year and that makes it possible, come spring, to contemplate planting tomatoes, yet again. Winter forgives us the crime of endlessly repeating ourselves.

We wait. That is what winter is. And without the wait, and without the emptiness, and without the browning and drying and blowing away, the cold, the frozen pots, the bareness, the shriveled herb leaves, the sticks of fig and rose, without the white pillows of snow, the spare horizon, spring would be nothing. How unbearable, a constant awakening, a continuous rising up, like remaining awake at a party that won't end. We need sleep. We need to be empty.

It is the only possible preparation for the excess to come.

DECEMBER MENU

Suddenly, there is time—to fill depressingly serious afternoons and drawn-out evenings with delicious smells. If the heat indoors becomes too much, all we have to do is crack open the door to the terrace for a slice of cold air to slide inside.

A winter menu is about earthiness and reassurance. Garlic pulled in summer and saved for just this moment, and sunchokes and pears that belong to the fall harvest usher in an oyster mushroom pizza—fragrant with terrace thyme—whose substantial crust and rich topping make one slice a satisfying midmeal event. The earth tones of the soup and main course are lifted by the bright crunch of radish-red and mustard-green in the salad.

Rhus Hour

Botanical joke. Staghorn sumac is *Rhus typhina*. And it is time to test our August infusion, whose clean tartness tastes good in a warm apartment on a freezing day.

⟪ MAKES ONE DRINK ⟫

3 ounces (6 tablespoons) sumac-infused vodka (see page 143)	2 ounces (4 tablespoons) dry vermouth	Strip of lemon zest

Shake up the vodka and vermouth with plenty of ice and strain into a coupe. Garnish with the lemon zest.

---

mid-winter supper

Rhus Hour

Creamy Garlic Soup

Sunchoke Salad

Mushroom Pizza

Pears Roasted in Red Wine with Bay Leaves

Creamy Garlic Soup

This soup makes excellent and unexpected use of garlic. The flavor is sweet and mellow, not stinky at all.

4 whole heads garlic (you read that correctly—4 heads), cloves separated

6 cups (1.4 L) chicken or vegetable stock

6 slices white bread, or 12 slices of yesterday's baguette, crusts trimmed off

1 cup (240 ml) crème fraîche or sour cream

Salt

Freshly ground black pepper

5 egg yolks, beaten

Add all the garlic cloves to a saucepan of water and bring to a boil, then reduce to a simmer and cook for 5 minutes. Pour the water off, pour in fresh water, and repeat. Pop the cloves from their skins and nip off the tough bit at the bottom of each.

In a large saucepan, heat the chicken or vegetable stock with the now-naked garlic. Bring to a simmer over medium heat and cook for 10 minutes. Add the bread, broken into pieces. Turn off the heat. Stir in the crème fraîche or sour cream. Stir to combine. In batches, puree the soup in a blender, pouring each finished batch into a waiting bowl. (If you would like a velvet-smooth soup, push it though a sieve after blending.)

Return the soup to the saucepan, taste for seasoning, and add salt and pepper. Add the beaten egg yolks. Heat the soup slowly and very carefully until it is hot but not simmering—if you boil it for even a moment, the eggs will curdle. Slow heat will cause them to thicken the soup and make it more velvety.

As a variation, brave guests might like to be served an intact egg yolk in each individual bowl of hot soup, to be stirred in at the table. In which case, add one more yolk to the recipe.

Sunchoke Salad

Sunchokes or Jerusalem artichokes are *Helianthus tuberosus*. They are native to eastern North America and an excellent garden plant—beautiful and edible. My mother used to grow them in Bloemfontein, in her terraced vegetable garden. I remember their tall yellow sunflowers against a warm brick wall. I hated the tubers then: a horrible, cruel substitute for potatoes, I thought, and a terrible disappointment when bitten into. Frauds. But we change. As a roasted vegetable they are sweet and creamy, but I love the raw tuber even more. Very crisp, slightly nutty, often sweet. Their season is October through March. They pair beautifully with the pepper of radishes and the bite of wintery mustard leaves.

⟪ SERVES SIX ⟫

FOR THE APPLE CIDER VINAIGRETTE

Salt

¼ teaspoon sugar

2 tablespoons apple cider vinegar

1 tablespoon yogurt

¼ cup (60 ml) walnut oil

Freshly ground black pepper

FOR THE SALAD

4 to 6 sunchokes, peeled

5 red or purple radishes, topped and tailed

1 Bosc pear, cored and sliced thinly

2 handfuls of small mustard leaves or other peppery microgreens

Make the vinaigrette: In a bowl or small jug, dissolve the salt and sugar in the vinegar. Add the yogurt, whisk with a fork, and then add the oil, whisking again until the vinaigrette emulsifies. Add pepper to taste.

Make the salad: Slice the sunchokes and radishes very, very thinly into rounds. Slice the cored pear lengthwise. Put the sunchokes, radishes, and pear in a large bowl.

Just before serving, toss the vegetables with some of the vinaigrette. Heap them in a salad bowl or on a serving plate. Toss the greens with what is left of the vinaigrette in the same bowl, and pile loosely on top of the vegetables. Lick your fingers if you like. The salad is ready.

Mushroom Pizza

Pizza cures nothing and delivers no one from evil, but eaten alone or in good company, it can help keep the boat afloat.

For this wild mushroom pizza I use a white, béchamel sauce base—I find tomato sauce too strong for the woodsy mushroom aroma. You can use many kinds of mushrooms for this; in October I use maitake, but even store-bought button mushrooms will taste good when given this treatment.

Pizza is an unusual main course, but cold weather oyster mushrooms are worth celebrating in this quintessentially American dish. All the elements of this recipe can be prepared ahead of time and assembled 25 minutes before you intend to eat the pie (as we call it in Brooklyn).

⪡ SERVES SIX ⪢

FOR THE PIZZA DOUGH
(see note)

1 cup (240 ml) warm water

1 tablespoon instant yeast

¼ teaspoon sugar

2 ¼ cups (315 g) flour

Large pinch of salt

FOR THE MUSHROOM TOPPING

3 tablespoons olive oil

3 cloves garlic, finely chopped

6 cups (420 g) cleaned and sliced oyster mushrooms

3 tablespoons lemon juice

Salt and freshly ground black pepper

Leaves from 6 sprigs fresh thyme

FOR THE CHEESE SAUCE

2 tablespoons plus 1 teaspoon unsalted butter

2 tablespoons flour

1 ½ cups (360 ml) warm milk

1 cup (100 g) finely grated Parmesan

Freshly ground black pepper

Freshly grated nutmeg

1 large ball (about 9 ounces / 260 g) fresh mozzarella

Note: This is a basic bread dough, and makes a Pullman-size loaf. I have also used it wrapped around a sausage meat filling to carry to a picnic, and for bread rolls. It is a perfect pizza dough, yielding a large, thick-crusted base. You may divide it in half if you want a thinner crust, but for these meaty mushrooms I like a hearty base that gives the mushrooms' flavor somewhere to go.

Make the pizza dough: Mix the water, yeast, sugar, and ½ cup (70 g) of the flour in a large bowl and stir very well until mixed. Cover and allow to proof for 10 minutes. Add the rest of the flour gradually, with the salt. When the dough is stiff, turn it onto a floured board and knead it until it feels smooth and silky, at least 10 minutes. Clean the bowl and lightly oil it, then return the dough to the bowl, cover, and set aside to rise until doubled in size.

Punch the dough back down.

If you are using a metal tray for baking, grease it. Place the dough in the middle of the tray and start pressing it outward toward the edges—I used the bunched middle joints of my right hand—always working from the middle of the dough and turning the tray as you go. (If you are a skilled pizza maker you may be able to stretch the dough in your hands, but I find that the pressing method works pretty well.) Keep at it until the dough has reached the edges of the tray, and leave a little collar around the lip, to catch any bubbling juices.

The dough may rest in the pan for 20 minutes to an hour.

Make the mushroom topping: In a wide saucepan over medium heat, heat 2 tablespoons of the oil. Add the mushrooms and cook until they exude liquid, about 6 minutes. Turn the heat up to high and allow the liquid to cook off. Continue to cook until the mushrooms begin to turn golden brown. Lower the heat to medium. Add the remaining 1 tablespoon oil and the garlic and cook gently until the garlic is translucent. Add the lemon juice, stir the mushrooms well, and allow the juice to cook off. Taste, and season with salt and pepper. Add the thyme leaves. Remove from the heat and allow to cool.

Make the cheese sauce: In a saucepan over medium-low heat, melt 2 tablespoons of the butter until foaming. Add the flour, whisking constantly. Lower the heat. Cook this roux for as long as you can stand, but for no less than 3 minutes. Add a splash of warm milk, and whisk briskly as the mixture seizes up and thickens. Add additional splashes of milk, whisking all the time to prevent lumps. Add the rest of the milk once you are certain that your mixture is smooth, and raise the heat to medium. Stir from time to time as the sauce thickens. Turn off the heat and add the Parmesan, stirring well to combine. Taste, and add pepper. (Salt may be unnecessary because of the cheese.) I like to add a whisper of nutmeg at this point.

Dot flecks of the remaining butter across the sauce's surface to help prevent a skin from forming. When the butter melts, tilt the pan slightly to allow it to spread thinly across the surface.

Assemble the pizza: Preheat the oven to 550°F (240°C) or as high as it can go. Hide the smoke alarm (remember to put it back later!).

Spread the cheese sauce thinly over the pizza dough. Cut the mozzarella into medium slices and halve each slice. Distribute the mozzarella slices evenly over the cheese sauce. Strew the mushrooms evenly across the top.

Slide the tray into the oven and cook until the crust is browning and crisp, 20 to 25 minutes.

Add fresh black pepper just before serving.

Pears Roasted in Red Wine with Bay Leaves

Everyone will be licking their fingers after tasting one of these spicy pears.

12 small pears
(or 6 large), peeled

2 cups (480 ml)
red wine

⅓ cup (65 g) sugar

10 black peppercorns

6 bay leaves

Preheat the oven to 350°F (180°C).

Halve and core the pears and arrange in a heavy pan or roasting dish. Add the wine, sugar, peppercorns, and bay leaves and place in the oven for 2 hours, occasionally spooning the wine over the pears.

Serve hot, or cool.

recipe index

Italic indicates subrecipe

acknowledgments

My thanks go to my agent, Carla Glasser, for her New York spirit: brief, and to the point. At Stewart, Tabori & Chang, to my kind editor, Dervla Kelly; managing editor Ivy McFadden, who made fine-combed sense out of the text, especially my recipes and measurements; and Leslie Stoker, for believing in this story enough to turn it into beautiful and increasingly threatened print. Thanks also to designer Anna Christian, for her dedication and skill.

To Stephen Orr, for his kindness and support along the way. To Johan van Zyl, whose story about *66 Square Feet* in *Visi Magazine* helped shape my seasonal approach to this book. To Melanie Hulse, for early advice and a sense of context. To Rick Darke, who emphasized authenticity in all things. To readers of the *66 Square Feet* blog, who were ready with opinions, encouragement, criticism, and considerable warmth.

To my parents, Henri and Maureen Viljoen, for giving me a beautiful life, and lots to think about.

To my husband, Vincent, who has tolerated (with grace) this book, a high-maintenance guest in a small space, which threatened to overstay its welcome: demanding attention at odd hours, and crying always for fresh-cut flowers, cold drinks, and multiple-course dinners. He has been a gentle voice of reason, has talked me down out of countless trees, and has been the source of a love that will never cease to astonish me. And for the photographs he contributed to this book, which capture the unexpected spirit of the city that I hoped to convey.

Finally, thanks to the custodians of the many green and wild spaces that this congested city contains. I accompany my gratitude with a plea that the City and State of New York fund and adequately staff the parks for which they are responsible.